THE
TOP
PRODUCER
LIFE

Build the

Real Estate

Career of

Your Dreams

in Any Economy

JASEN EDWARDS

THE TOP PRODUCER LIFE
Copyright © 2021 Jasen Edwards

The information presented herein represents the view of the author as of the date of publication. This book is presented for informational purposes only. Neither the author nor the publisher is engaged in rendering legal, accounting, or other professional services. If legal advice or other expert assistance is required, the services of a competent professional person should be sought.

Cover and interior design: www.DominiDragoone.com
Editorial services: Sandra Wendel, www.SandraWendel.com
Cover image © Doug Ellis Photography, www.DougEllis.com

ISBN (print): 978-1-7364952-0-9
ISBN (ebook): 978-1-7364952-1-6
ISBN (audiobook) 978-1-7364952-2-3

Published by Jabari Life, LLC
www.JasenEdwards.com
Contact the author at hello@JasenEdwards.com.

▼

To access all of the free bonus material, including
the Perfect Client Worksheet, go to:

JASENEDWARDS.COM/TPLBONUS

Contents

Part II: Working with Business Macros

Part III Living Your Top Producer Life

1

▼

From Teenager to Top Producer: An Introduction to the Top Producer Life

August 27, 1996. That is the day I unexpectedly discovered my professional passion.

I was a year and a half into my real estate career and felt like a complete failure. I only had two small sales in that amount of time, which brought in approximately $6,000 in commissions. That was after the split to my broker, but before taxes and expenses. I was twenty-one and had been living off the good graces of my parents who, seeing no future for me as an agent, gave me the ultimatum I knew was coming: "You've tried real estate, now go back to college or get a real job."

The problem was I didn't want to do either. I hated college and had no clue what I wanted to do with my life. Real estate was something I did because, when I worked at the Texas Association of Realtors in high school, everyone around me convinced me I'd be successful at sales. So when I turned eighteen, I got my license. Even though I wasn't any good at selling, I liked the business and really didn't want to give up.

But at that point I felt I had no choice and took a job at a record store called Camelot Music located in a shopping mall. The mall was brand new and wouldn't be open for another two weeks so I had time to kill before having to clock in for my first shift. During those two weeks, my life in real estate progressed as usual. I didn't have any clients or prospects, but I did have plenty of lunches and happy hours to attend.

I was living the joke that "you can go broke in real estate but not hungry." It's really true that there is food around every corner. I did my best to act as if everything was normal, and because nearly all agents are self-employed, I didn't have to tell anyone that I'd quit. The truth is that I was embarrassed I had to get a job and grateful my predicament was so easy to hide from everyone. Everyone except my broker.

I never told her explicitly that I'd taken the job at the mall, but she must have figured it out. I'm certain she recognized a behavior pattern in me she'd no doubt seen many times before. One day, she approached me in the hall and asked if I was going to go to the free training event she'd arranged for us. This was going to be a special company-wide event that took the place of the regular sales meeting, so you better believe I was going. Events like that had wonderful catering—think free brunch.

The event was August 27, 1996, and, as I said, it changed the direction of my life.

After stuffing my face at the buffet, I took my seat and began listening to the trainer who'd flown in to take us through a half-day seminar. She was also there to sell us on enrolling in the full twelve-week program she would come back to teach. Immediately I knew this was going to be the event that saved me. I wrote down every word that came out of the trainer's mouth and was more excited than I'd ever been about real estate.

But at the end of the seminar, I faced two new challenges: the tuition was nearly $1,000, which I didn't have and couldn't get, and training was going to start on the day I was supposed to begin work at Camelot Music. Talk about an emotional roller coaster. I went from an extreme high during the session to driving home in tears. I almost wished I hadn't gone because at least then I wouldn't have known what I was going to be missing.

Then, just one day before the full program was to start, my broker approached me again and insisted I take a loan from her to go through the course. She told me I'd pay her back over my next two commissions, and, frankly, I was thrilled she believed in me enough to trust I'd have two more commissions.

I poured myself into the course for three months and did everything I was asked to do without question. Time went by so fast I didn't even realize until graduation that I'd outproduced everyone and generated $60,000 in commissions. I was only twenty-one when I completed that course, and at that time I honestly couldn't tell the difference between $60,000 and $6 million. All I can tell you was that I felt rich.

From then on, I sold real estate in Austin, Texas, for over thirteen years and, in those days, was the youngest person ever listed on the *Austin Business Journal's* Top 50 agents list. From the outside, I had a stunning career, but the real secret was that I wasn't passionate about selling real estate. I loved selling and the money was good because I got really good at it, but real estate itself wasn't that exciting to me.

Eventually, I began to explore what I really discovered at that half-day seminar over a decade earlier—my love of speaking and coaching. You see, what excited me most as I sat in the audience had nothing to do with real estate. It was the trainer's performance as a speaker. It took many years for me to connect the dots, but one day it hit me that I'd become the guy everyone else in the office turned to for advice. Every day, if I was in the office, other agents would line up to ask me what-do-you-do-when questions: "Hey, Jasen, what do you do when a seller says this—?"

When I realized that I would naturally spend hours helping these other agents for free, I decided the time had come to learn to coach professionally. I went back to the organization that taught me how to sell real estate and learned how to be a speaker and a coach.

These days, I've been working with salespeople for longer than I sold real estate, and no matter where I go or what the market is like when I get there, I've noticed agents struggling with the same things I did when I began my career. It's what inspires me to get out of bed every day, enthusiastic about working with others who, like me, don't want to get a "real job" but, instead, want to realize the vision they had in their mind when they first earned their real estate license.

That vision is what I call the Top Producer Life, and although it looks a bit different for each person, you deserve to be living your version, and I'm going to show you how.

2

▼

What Nobody Tells You about Real Estate (but I Will)

Before we start building your Top Producer Life, you deserve to be told the hard truth. I'm not suggesting that people lie to you when you get started, but I do believe people in leadership don't want to discourage you. There is so much pressure to recruit new talent, it's easier for those in a recruiting role to gloss over the more difficult topics and hope for the best as you discover everything on your own in the real estate business.

My intention isn't to discourage you either, but I'm also not trying to recruit you. And looking back, my first few years would have been much easier if someone had sat me down and given me a heads-up on a few truths. So here they are.

First, you should know that for most agents, the first commission usually doesn't show up for three to six months. New agents enter the business with a desire to control their own schedule only to find themselves in a constant state of low-grade panic about the next commission and end up working seven days a week to get money coming in.

On top of that, because everything is optional when you are self-employed, most agents unconsciously block their own success. I say unconsciously because no one wakes up and declares they'll be unsuccessful. But without proper guidance, it's easy to get stuck making decisions on a daily basis that quickly lead to failure. Decisions like not prospecting or not working on your mindset don't feel too consequential on any single day. However, when strung together day after day, it's essentially the same as flat out declaring you're going to fail.

One huge flaw in the licensing process is that finding clients is rarely discussed. So unless the brokerage you join has a world-class sales training program, then you're left to figure out how you'll get clients on your own. You may know how to fill out a contract, but almost no one comes into the business knowing how to generate leads and convert them to appointments consistently. That requires real sales skill, and many agents are deathly afraid of being seen as a salesperson.

Most of the training that is readily available in the beginning is hyper-focused on company systems and the mechanics of transactions. But if you are walking around scared to death of what others think, that training is going to be useless. Worse than that, when people don't get their fear of being seen as a salesperson under control, their income suffers, and because of that, they end up putting pressure on their clients just to make some money. In other words, in an attempt to avoid being seen as pushy, they actually become pushy.

You should also know that most people who come into real estate don't know how to be self-employed, and there aren't many places to learn that specific skill set. Many people come into real estate from corporate America, and one of the reasons the business is so attractive is because people love the idea of controlling their own schedule. If you have an entrepreneurial spirit and have had to ask for permission to leave early to pick up your child, the allure of being your own boss is very real.

Unfortunately, the industry does almost nothing to show you how to be your own boss. For many agents, whatever feels the most urgent in any given moment is where their attention goes, whether it's good for business or not.

Another aspect that isn't discussed nearly enough in the beginning is how much you must learn. The truth is, after the education to get a license ends, the real education begins.

In addition to learning how to use company systems and get through a transaction itself, you must learn how to market yourself, generate leads, and deal with rejection. Once you start generating leads, you'll have to learn to persuade prospects to schedule appointments. From there you must learn to control your appointments, negotiate your commission, ask for signatures, and handle objections.

You'll also have to learn to maintain a connection with past clients over long periods of time so that you bring in referrals and repeat business. You'll have to learn so much more about the systems of a home, lending, surveys, and title insurance than is ever discussed in licensing school. And because you are a business owner, you'll have to learn how to handle negative reviews online, how to maintain your personal safety when meeting strangers, and how to deal with emotions from stressed-out clients.

Then there are your emotions. To live the life of a top producer, you'll have to develop a thick skin. If you ever felt rejected as a kid or were made to feel you weren't worthy of success, corresponding emotions are going to rear their ugly head soon after entering the world of the self-employed. At some point, everyone will experience bouts of anxiety, self-doubt, frustration, self-consciousness, and fear, just to name a few. Of course there will be feelings of extreme satisfaction, happiness, accomplishment, and fulfillment, but no one talks about what triggers the negative emotions.

For most people, it's a series of firsts that catches them off-guard: The first time you're told no when asking for an appointment. The first time you lose a client to another agent. The first time a deal doesn't close or a client fires you. The first time you have to give a presentation to a stranger or handle a commission objection from someone you considered a friend. The first time your family member hires another agent. The first time someone leaves a negative review about you online. The first time your spouse or kids become angry with you because they don't understand why you aren't with them all weekend. Geez, why doesn't anyone tell us this while we are going through real estate school?

It's no secret that the real estate industry has a high turn-over rate. You see, agents quit real estate all the time. But unlike quitting a job in corporate America, they don't leave right away. Instead, they mentally quit after having progressively given up over the course of about eighteen months.

If you've been around a while, you've seen it. An agent who has mentally quit is present but never busy. He's the first person busy agents turn to for help with open houses. He shows up at every industry event that has food but never seems to have a client. Then one day, after a lot of pain and a drained savings account, when he has literally no other option, he takes the paycheck job and sneaks out the back door.

This was my life in the beginning. The industry makes it super easy to hang around with no immediate repercussions for not producing. The equivalent lack of production in corporate America will get you fired—but not in real estate. It's my observation that people who spend about eighteen months in the business without building any momentum end up emotionally drained and are suffering from a drained bank account. It's at this point that most have literally run out of cash and are facing lots of pressure from their spouse to get a real job. It's never easy to give up on a dream, and people tend to hang on as long as they possibly can. It's why the quitting process drags out until that twenty-fourth month when it's time to renew the license.

The cost of continuing education, license renewal fees to the state, and annual association dues are usually the triggers for an agent to finally admit defeat and move on. Now that I've said it, you'll see this pattern all the time: quit at eighteen months, physically leave at twenty-four. I've heard it said that real estate is too easy to get into, and that may be, but it's a humbling hit to the ego when an unsuccessful person leaves.

But here's the great part: you don't have to worry about any of this. It's important to be aware of what I just covered, but not worried. Someone came along and showed me how to live the life of a top producer, and you can learn how as well. It doesn't matter if this is day one or day 1,001 of your career.

Let's go a little deeper. Would you say you're ready for the life of a top producer? If you're thinking you are, you'd be normal, but clearly something is going on that we should examine, because so few people ever realized the vision in their head when they decided to get a license.

Therefore, I'm going to take you through a self-analysis that will help you determine where you are now so that as you work through the book, you can lean in to the areas where you need the most improvement. I created this analysis after hundreds of recruiting appointments and countless hours coaching people over the years. As you read through this set of questions, pretend we're in a private coaching session. My role is to help you see into blind spots so that you become hyper-aware of where you stand. From that point, it's much easier to chart a clear path forward and find inspiration to keep going.

Take the top producer readiness analysis and ask yourself these questions:

Can you clearly articulate why you want a successful career in real estate sales?

People don't always realize real estate is just as tough and risky as any other kind of business. When asked why someone wants to get into the business, the most common three responses are these: I like houses, I like working with people, and I want to control my own schedule. That's understandable but it's just not enough.

First, houses have nothing to do with the actual job of an agent. Second, people aren't always nice; and third, almost no one in real estate does an effective job at controlling their own schedule. So when adversity strikes, what's going to keep you going? The allure has to be big enough to outweigh the pains and adversities of building a client-facing service business. Your *why* has to be so big that rejection is more desirable to you than not succeeding.

Barbara Corcoran of the hit show *Shark Tank*, who got her start in the real estate business, often says that her most successful agents were always the ones with something to prove.

Are you financially prepared?

When people get into real estate, most don't have anywhere near the amount of time they think they have to build momentum. As I mentioned, it's not uncommon for an agent to go six months before receiving their first commission and two years before commissions become steady—and by steady I mean at least one per month.

Ideally you would have six months of living expenses in savings and several thousand dollars more available to invest in marketing and lead generation activities. If you don't have that, a side hustle or a part-time job may be necessary. There's no shame in having multiple sources of income, but remember that real estate is a demanding business, so if you're starting short on cash, do everything you can to save up a six-month cushion so you can drop side gigs that will slow your development.

Are you clear about your primary job?

A career in real estate obviously has a lot to do with housing, but so many people struggle, or ride the income roller coaster at best, because they fail to learn that their primary job is to generate leads. If they do their job well, the reward is a listing or a new buyer client. All of the things people typically identify with as the job of an agent is really just the reward side of the equation.

When you are an independent contractor, you are just like any other small business owner. For example, attorneys with their own law practice may love to argue in court, but they will only get to do that if they have first done their job, which is to find people who need their services. That's called lead generation. If the primary job was taking care of a client, then at the end of every transaction, agents, attorneys, and any self-employed person would have a steady stream of clients lined up. But we all know that's not what happens.

Most self-employed service industry professionals ride the income roller coaster because they lack this basic awareness. And I suppose that would be okay if every transaction was so huge that once you got paid you could afford to wait 90 to 120 days for the next commission, but that is also not the case for the majority of people.

Are you willing to take proactive control of your schedule?

One of the statements I made earlier was that people aren't really taught to be self-employed, and there is nowhere that truth shows up more clearly than how low-producing agents use their time. There was a day when most professionals got up, went to their office, and for the most part did their work, then went about their life.

Without smartphones and social media, it was obvious to everyone when you were wasting time. If you were hanging around the office screwing off, everyone knew it, and every once in a while, a top producer would get irritated enough to say something like, "Are you guys going to eat title company donuts all day or try to find a buyer for my listing?"

Today it's possible to sit at a desk and tap around on a smartphone for hours, and no one will really know if you're working or wasting time. And every day, fewer and fewer brokers maintain desks for agents anyway. We have lost a layer of structure in the office environment that used to help us maintain a bit of discipline. Now we're in a "tap-tap-scroll and react" environment. People who get into real estate with the dream of controlling their own schedule rarely control anything. Instead, they wake up and react. React to the smartphone alarm, react to the emails they look at with blurry vision while still in bed, react to the images on social media, to what they see on the news, to what honey and the kids did or didn't do on the way out the door, to the person who cut them off on the way to Starbucks, to the other agent who doesn't seem to cooperate.

I could make the rest of this book a ridiculous list of activities that make us feel like we're working but that, at the end of the day, does nothing to advance us toward our goals. Top producers have figured out how to regain control of what they do with their time. Every day? Not a chance; but most days, definitely.

Are you willing to fully own your role as a salesperson?

At its core, the fear of being seen as a salesperson is triggered by an overabundance of concern about what others think of you. To make matters worse, if you ever had an authority figure make a disparaging comment about a salesperson when you were a child, on some level the emotion that goes along with that exists in your subconscious mind, often very well hidden.

To be sure, I see people all the time get into the business and attempt to avoid the salesperson label by calling themselves consultants or advisors. Now, on a logical level, I believe everyone truly understands they are salespeople, but we don't overcome fear with logic. You can see evidence of that by looking at how people project their own fears onto others. If you think salespeople are sleazy, you've most likely convinced yourself that everyone thinks the same way. The story in your head is literally imposing your world view onto everyone else with an almost stubborn insistence that they must see the world in the same way. Not very logical is it?

Sales at its highest level is a kind of leadership, and to become masterful at it, you must treat it as an art form. This means you'll study salesmanship for the rest of your career, and in a business like real estate, because every transaction is different, you'll never run out of opportunities to reach new levels of understanding.

You've probably heard some people referred to as born salespeople, and I would agree there are born salespeople out there, but I was definitely not one. In fact, most people are not born to sell; the majority of us have to learn, and we can get just as good at selling as those for whom it comes naturally. It's just like any other art form. For example, music is considered a fine art yet has a ton of rules you must learn. The piano restricts you to 88 keys, 44 black and 44 white. To play, you must make use of two lines on sheet music, the base and treble lines, and you only have so many notes. If you're going to be good at playing the piano, you must accept and learn these rules, and once you do, you'll spend the rest of your life practicing with those rules to become a masterful pianist.

Sales works the same way. A few people are the equivalent of Mozart, and then there are the rest of us who must learn the structure and rules of salesmanship.

Are you willing to proactively control your mindset?

Looking back I suppose I had to become a coach. What else would I have been given that I started reading Zig Ziglar's book *See You at the Top* as a six-year-old. I don't remember words like *mindset* or *affirmations* from my childhood, but I was certainly exposed early on.

One of my earliest memories is of an afternoon at my dad's apartment after he and my mother divorced. For lunch he made my brother and me soup. After cleaning up, he asked us to take the labels off of our cans while he set stacks of magazines with scissors, tape, and glue on the table. He helped us cut the eyeballs off the people in the magazines, and, for a six-year-old boy, that was a super fun thing to do with my dad and brother.

I mutilated the people in the magazines until I had a large stack of eyeballs. When we had enough, we taped and glued the eyeballs to the outside of the can, effectively creating new labels. After that my dad put strips of paper on the table and asked us to write out what we wanted to be, do, or have. I remember saying I wanted a new bike, and my dad's reply was to write, "I can have a new bike." Since I was only six, he helped me write what I couldn't, and we kept going until we filled the can with these strips of paper that held the desires of a young boy.

Every morning I was with him, we'd start the day by grabbing my I CAN (eye can) and pull out a strip of paper. My dad would ask me to reflect on the phrase on the paper throughout the day. So if it said, "I can have a new bike," he wanted me to think that I could have a new bike all day long. He was teaching me how to think successfully. He was teaching me about affirmations. If he'd used the word *affirmation*, I probably wouldn't have understood, but an I CAN was easy for the mind of a kid.

Maybe I was lucky, maybe it was fate, but when I became a coach, it became clear pretty quickly that most people I'd work with did not have this kind of influence early on. As you'll see, controlling your mindset proactively goes way beyond affirmations, but you have to be willing to take control in the first place.

Are you willing to make mistakes?

People who need to know everything before they do anything are simply expressing their own fear of failure. One powerful defense mechanism is education. By this I mean classroom education. Sitting in a class provides the illusion of work with the benefit of not having to do anything. There are endless classes to take in real estate, and it's not uncommon to see an agent with no real track record of their own, and who isn't making any money, volunteer to teach a class for free.

Learning from a mentor or in a classroom environment is never complete without action, so you'll always see a top producer matching their time in a class or seminar or coaching with lots of time in the field taking action. And they make a ton of mistakes. True learning happens on the other side of failure. When you understand that, you no longer fear failure because, without it, there is no growth.

Think of it this way. From the moment your license is active, you have a real estate practice. Every client you ever have will allow you an opportunity to practice your craft, just like every patient a doctor has gives them an opportunity to practice their craft. We all know doctors make mistakes and you will too. In fact, everyone who has a professional practice of any kind will, by definition, make mistakes. If not, you'd have a real estate perfect, and your doctor would have a medical perfect—not a practice. Sounds ridiculous when I put it that way, doesn't it?

So are you willing?

Anyone who's been in real estate sales for five minutes knows what critics mean when they suggest we agents should get a real job. To be clear, I think selling real estate is a real job and one of the most important in our entire economy. But nobody working hard to build the life of their dreams wants to hear a loved one suggest out of fear that they give up and get a job with a regular paycheck. So how you responded to those questions is important. Together, they lead to the prerequisites for living the Top Producer Life.

If you can state clearly why you're in real estate, if you are financially prepared or willing to hustle until you are, and if you are willing to accept that your primary job is to generate leads, then you are on the right track. In addition, if you are willing to proactively control your schedule and your mindset, you're even closer to success.

Finally, if you are willing to do all of that and practice salesmanship without beating yourself up when you make a mistake, then your visions will certainly be realized. Of course, being willing is one thing and knowing how is another. Early on I was willing to do anything I could to avoid going back to college or to work at the record store. As long as it was legal, I was down. But I didn't know how, and there's nothing more frustrating than knowing what you should be doing but not knowing how to do it.

In the rest of this book, I will be your coach. I will teach you how to build your Top Producer Life.

Part I

Building the Business You Always Dreamed of Having

3

▼

Business Macros Explained: The Secret Formula for Achieving Top Producer Status

As I started working with agents, my focus was on helping them balance their business activities in much the same way we might balance our diet. It didn't take long to learn that nearly all agents follow a predictable path of growth and experience equally predictable challenges as they build their career.

Along that path are three areas of focus that encompass all of the smaller items agents work to improve. So rather than work with agents on a list of hundreds of individual skills, I chose to focus them on these three areas I introduce in this chapter. Over time, I made the bet that we'd get to all of the individual skills while keeping their career in balance. And it totally worked.

The results: New agents got their business off the ground in record time. Experienced agents got more efficient and unlocked new levels of production and satisfaction. Many agents reported enjoying their work again after years of feeling unbalanced and uninspired, and one of my clients even ended up on the cover of *Realtor* magazine.

Now, after more than twenty years of selling and coaching, I'm able to say confidently that everyone who succeeds in real estate gives appropriate time and energy to three areas of focus: their mindset, their sales methodologies, and their marketing tactics. I call those three areas business macros, and they comprise a three-part solution to achieving all you envisioned when you earned your license.

Business Macro One: Mindset

The mindset macro is the most important of the three and—even though it's getting better—still the most ignored. Without a healthy mindset, it makes no difference how good you are at selling or how many leads your marketing brings in; your business is going to be in serious danger if you don't pay attention in this area.

To be sure, the most common call I get as a coach is not for help improving a sales skill or a marketing tactic. When people reach out to me initially, it's usually because their attitude is in the gutter and they need a kick in the butt. They know their business is in trouble and are experiencing feelings of worry, anxiety, fear, even depression, and they can't see a way forward on their own. Can you imagine if I took a person in that state and said, "Okay, so let's work on your listing presentation."

In business the mindset macro is made up of your belief systems, which are built upon a set of thoughts consistently repeated in your mind on a daily basis. In other words, your beliefs are the story going on inside your head. We all have an internal story, and it's either supporting our life as a top producer or preventing it.

Perhaps the most extreme example of a detrimental mindset I've ever seen came along just a few years after I began coaching for the same program that saved my own career. One of my clients was a brokerage in Nashville. I was excited about their program because it was going to be one of my largest to date. There were around seventy agents enrolled, and the energy would be off the charts in the classroom sessions because many of the agents were retired from the country music industry. But I quickly learned they were still entertainers at heart.

During the week between the initial kickoff and session one, I got a call from a very upset agent while I was at the gym. The agent wanted to know if she could get a refund for the course. I told her if she went through the first session and didn't like the program at that point, she could have a full refund. That answer triggered extreme anger, and the agent began yelling at me so loudly that people around me in the gym were staring. My hands were tied because that was the policy of the training company, and as one of their trainers, I couldn't change it.

As you can imagine, on the morning of session one, I was on the lookout for this angry person. The first session is always a bit hectic. There are materials to pass out, students who are enrolling at the last minute, and generally just a lot of admin work that goes along with actual instruction.

As the morning went on, momentum took over, and I never spoke to the angry agent. I didn't know what she looked like, so I started to think she didn't bother coming. But on the first break, she approached me and grabbed my hand as she introduced herself. Before I even had a chance to react, she said in front of everyone, and I'm paraphrasing here,

"Thank you for what you said this morning. My family is in bankruptcy, and you are going to help get us out of it. I'm not leaving the program."

You could have heard a pin drop as she hugged me and walked off. Her broker leaned over to me and, after picking up her jaw from the floor, told me the agent was the top producing agent in the entire state of Tennessee. Before that moment, none of us knew she had filed for bankruptcy. Her initial impulse was to enroll in the training, then she freaked out about money and screamed at me on the phone before ultimately settling in and doing the work.

Now, think this through. At that very moment she was the statewide top producer, which meant she had plenty of money coming in the door, but because her mindset was completely messed up, she lost money as fast as she earned it. During our eight weeks together, she fine-tuned her sales skills, but her biggest improvement was in her mindset. About six months after graduation, she was happy and thriving again and has not had to face bankruptcy since.

Business Macro Two: Sales Methodologies

As you've no doubt noticed, this isn't a traditional business book, and I'm not going to be discussing accounting or leadership and management, which could easily come to mind when I mention the word *methodology.*

Instead, we are going to talk about sales methodologies because, first, you are obviously a salesperson, and, second, in any business, no one else gets a job until a product or service sells. I've always found it a bit strange that society tends to hold a higher opinion of professional disciplines such as finance or management when, in fact, there are no numbers to count and no employees to lead unless a talented salesperson gets out there and sells for the company.

Employees who work in administration-type roles—as important as they are to the bigger picture—owe their jobs to the creators and the salespeople in their companies. Yet we have terms like *used car salesman* that unfortunately persist and indicate the level of disrespect still suffered by salespeople. Our society's collective resistance to honoring the profession of sales like we do others such as finance or marketing is a large reason people struggle on an individual level when entering sales.

This is the most misunderstood and the most feared of the business macros. The weight of the baggage carried by individuals and the collective around salesmanship obscures its true importance and significance. Sales methodologies are how you build your practice. And all you have to do is look at the turnover rate in real estate to understand that an agent could have a million followers on Instagram, but without the ability to sell, their career dies.

To be clear, marketing and sales are different and yet often confused. Marketing in a real estate practice is what you do to bring in a lead and/or raise awareness of your brand. We'll talk more about this, but for now, it's important to understand that marketing doesn't get you very far without strong sales methodologies. I could run an award-winning ad campaign that brings you tons of leads, but if you don't know how to handle them, it's just a bunch of wasted time and money.

For about three years I worked with a medium-sized independent real estate firm, and my job was to redesign their training department. When I started, training consisted of an informal and inconsistent string of classes taught by whichever willing and able agent was available to talk on the subject. Sometimes the sessions worked well, but often they did not. This was a huge problem because the brokerage was spending a significant amount of money each month—tens of thousands of dollars—on marketing to generate leads for the agents. The leads were definitely coming in, but unless those leads literally said to an agent, "Come list my house" or "Take me to buy a house," the potential customers were being ignored.

So I created a new career path the company could use as a training platform to nurture agents from the day they got licensed until the day they were living the life of a top producer. The portion of the system that received the most attention was the core sales training program. After agents spent some time getting their business off the ground and building momentum, they were allowed to enroll in a program that would focus heavily on developing their sales skills. We studied fifty-two agents who went through the training. After the first year, they generated $1,035,000 more commission dollars (after their split) than they had the year before.

Another reason I believe there is such resistance around working on improving sales methodologies is because the process is slow and frustrating. In real estate it takes at least two years before you start to feel as if you really know what should happen next in a transaction. Sales is an artistic discipline, and you don't learn solely from a book or a class. You have to be willing to go out and fall on your face at times.

The good news you have to learn only a few methodologies to get really good at selling, and they aren't that complicated. For example, you'll learn a simple and powerful methodology that you will use to schedule appointments with prospective clients and another that you'll use to turn a prospect into a client. When you begin to understand this business macro, you'll never again question what to do next with a prospect or client. This would be a good time to let you know I'm not a script guy. Scripts have their place in sales, but the world has moved on from how most people are taught to use a canned sales pitch in favor of a more authentic approach. Consumers will know immediately if you are using a script because you won't sound authentic or even remotely like yourself. I thought I could get away with that when I was learning to sell, but even back then, my trainer was a fan of using scripts only for a short period of time while we were learning the power of the underlying methodology.

To suggest you could learn a defined set of scripts that you put on repeat in your interactions with clients assumes that every client is exactly the same. I quickly learned they aren't, and they never seemed to have their lines anyway. So if the idea of repeating a script makes you want to puke, you're in luck, we aren't going there. In fact, you'll learn to sell in a way that allows your special and unique qualities to shine from the very beginning.

Think of sales methodologies like train travel. If I wanted to travel on a train from Los Angeles to San Diego, there would be a track. No matter what kind of train was used, as long as it stayed on the track, it would get to San Diego. You may like riding on vintage coal-fired trains, and I may like modern high-speed trains, but in both cases, the track is still taking us to San Diego.

The methodologies you will learn are going to be described with the same train track analogy. Humans don't evolve quickly, which means we have had a very long time to learn how we behave in various situations, including interactions with salespeople. This is good for your business because it means that you can follow a track that keeps you in alignment with your client or prospect at every step. The words you use can be authentically yours, not someone else's (a script), and as long as you stay on track, you'll still get the result you need.

Business Macro Three: Marketing Tactics

Marketing and advertising tactics make up the third business macro. This is the least important of the three macros and, even so, is given the most inappropriate amounts of time and energy. Now let's get this out of the way up front. I did not just say marketing is not important. It is in fact very important. Marketing is critical for your business. It may seem like I'm picking on it here because often, when I first meet an agent, they are way off balance. Either they aren't marketing their services consistently or they are relying too heavily on this business macro. It's easy to see why too much focus is often given to marketing.

First, marketing can be fun and often feeds the ego. Just look around and notice what you see in the industry when it comes to marketing. Not only is there a ton of it, nearly all of it is focused on agent promotion.

When I was a young salesperson, a company would create what they called a "slogo"—a combination of the words *slogan* and *logo*. Agents in my office would pay between $5,000 and $10,000 to have a logo created and a slogan to go along with it. The company would take a professional picture of the agent leaning on a neutral surface, photoshop out the background,

and place the agent over one of the letters in their name with a tagline, the slogan, below it.

All of that together would create an image that agents would use as their brand logo, and they'd order a huge marketing package to go along with it. Business cards, stationery, yard signs, you name it. Looking back it was so over the top and ridiculous, but I'd be lying if I told you I didn't want a "slogo" myself.

Over the years photoshop became less expensive and digital design services became more common. I was given the nickname "agentjason" by the agents in my office, and once I could afford it, I played with the idea of creating a slogo around my nickname. I even had some mockups done. But in the end, I never finished the project. By that time I'd discovered marketing genius Seth Godin who was conditioning my mind to make my marketing more about the client, and less about me. But Seth and his millions of book sales be damned, it's still really hard for agents to resist the pull of personal promotion in marketing. It just makes our ego feel so good to have our name and face out there.

People pay so much attention to marketing because it's easier than facing rejection from another human. It also gives the illusion of doing important work. Rather than do the task that promotes professional growth, like active prospecting, it's far easier to screw around with a Facebook page. But marketing tactics simply aren't a solid foundation upon which to build a business. Only principles can give you that, and those take more guidance, discipline, and time to master. Sorry—not very sexy or ego boosting, I know.

To be sure, another common call I get from past clients is a request for help getting back to the basics. Here's what that means: they've gotten too distracted by marketing. The first time I can remember this happening to me was when I was at a trade show and a vendor was selling business cards on CD-ROM.

Picture a CD with the top and bottom portions cut off and shrunk down a bit so it looked like a business card with the left and right sides curved like a CD. They looked so cool in the demonstration. The company printed my picture and contact information on the front and it came in a protective sleeve. The best part was the movie on the CD that showed pictures of me, my past clients, testimonials, images of homes I'd sold, and a professional voice-over of my bio. It was super cool and very expensive, but I ordered a ton of them.

And the first week they arrived, I sent them out. Sadly, one of my new clients called to complain that it got stuck in his laptop drive and cost him hundreds of dollars to have removed.

I call situations like this "falling into the try-this trap." The try-this trap is waiting for you everywhere, and it's most evident in your email inbox. Each of the seemingly nonstop marketing emails promises to be the magic solution to all your problems. *Try this and you'll have unlimited leads. Try this and you'll only have to work four hours a week. Try this and you'll get 100k followers on social media.* It's like walking into a bakery and seeing rows of cookies and cakes and muffins and scones. Each one is screaming out to you, try me I'm yummy.

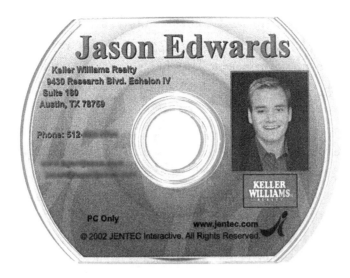

Baked goods are my weakness and you know what? Each one I pick up tastes wonderful on the first bite. But by the third bite, I'm wishing I never started. See the parallel I'm drawing here? If you don't like baked goods, just fill in the blank with your vice. Maybe you can't resist candy or chocolate. One friend of mine wouldn't eat a donut if his life depended on it but is powerless against the temptations of frozen yogurt.

Effective marketing requires consistency and discipline. That idea flies in the face of the instant gratification society we live in currently. I'm not suggesting you never try a new marketing tactic, but you have to be aware of how easily such gimmicks can become a trap when combined with a lack of patience and consistency. There's an evil saying out there that goes like this: if you can't make any money selling real estate, you can always earn a lot selling to agents. They'll always try something new. This, along with the typical agent's aggressive avoidance of even a hint of rejection, is why you see such an inappropriate focus on marketing tactics.

IIFYM (If It Fits Your Macros), the Secret Formula

I can teach you how to fit cookies and cake into your diet and maintain six pack abs just like I can teach you to incorporate marketing tactics without going completely off track in your business. The acronym IIFYM comes from the fitness world and it's the answer to one basic question: Can I eat this? The answer is always, yes, if it fits your macros. The concept originated with a desire to break away from highly restrictive diets that few people complied with for very long—low carbs, no carbs, no fat, only low fat—you get the idea.

Just like my fitness coach gave me guidance on how much of my diet should be protein, carbs, and fat, here is the mix of business macros I secretly used for years to help people build their own Top Producer Life. Let's look at them in the context of a six-day workweek:

- ▶ 40% Mindset: 3.2 hours per day or 19.2 per week
- ▶ 35% Sales Methodology: 2.8 hours per day or 16.8 per week
- ▶ 25% Marketing Tactics: 2 hours per day or 12 per week

If I can convince you to work toward those percentages, you should experience dramatic improvements just like my clients who didn't even know I was using them as guidance behind the scenes. I'm not saying it's going to be easy at first to hit those numbers, but I am suggesting it's that simple. This is your secret formula to living the Top Producer Life.

You may struggle at first on your journey, but you will master your business macros eventually. The rest of this book is devoted to helping you do just that.

Part II

Working with Business Macros

4

Mindset Macro:
The Foundation for Life
as a Top Producer

Now that you understand the importance of the business macros, the next three chapters will explain each in depth. So let's
dig into specific ways you can work with the mindset macro to
design and maintain your Top Producer Life. First, we'll look
at the topic of mindset from a broader perspective and how
it affects your life overall. Then we'll narrow down to specific
applications in your business. Once you've got a good handle
on the big picture, it becomes much easier to maintain a powerful mindset on a daily basis.

Affirmations and Law of Attraction: You Get What You Think about Whether You Want It or Not

When my dad guided me to make an eye can (I CAN), he
never used the word *affirmation* because I wouldn't have

understood it at the age of six. Many of the adults I've worked with don't even have a complete understanding of affirmations either.

During training sessions, when I ask an audience to give me their definition, I always get responses like a positive statement or an encouraging phrase, but that's only part of it. Affirmation comes from the verb to affirm and the most basic definition is to state as fact or to assert strongly and publicly. Most people think of affirmations as concepts rather than actions and haven't considered that you can affirm negativity just as easily as you can affirm positivity.

You've probably heard the phrase "speak it into existence," and truth be told, you can speak anything into existence. In fact, you are always speaking your reality into existence whether you're conscious of it or not.

I remember when my understanding of this expanded beyond the lessons of my father. It was the early 2000s, and a coworker was taking me to the airport in Tampa. These were the early years of my work as a speaker and coach, and rather than listen to the radio, he asked if I'd be willing to listen to a CD from an author he liked who went by the name Abraham-Hicks. Before he hit play, he warned me that it would sound strange at first, even a bit like a cult but asked me to give it a shot and not judge what I heard too quickly.

Just like he promised, the narrative started off pretty weird. I heard the speaker take a deep breath and say good morning to which the audience chanted back good morning as if they were in church. Definitely not the kind of motivational speaking I was into at the time, but I thought it was funny and listened politely because I didn't want my friend to think I was judging him.

The more the woman spoke, the more her speech patterns normalized and she began to make a lot of sense. Then, out of nowhere she said one line that punched me in the gut unexpectedly. She said, "You get what you think about whether you want it or not."

Such a simple little statement that today I easily embrace, but then it was like the universe reached inside of me and cracked open an awareness that was impossible to ignore or deny. It was also an awareness I was not yet ready to face. I could immediately sense the truth of that statement, and at the time it terrified me.

Looking back I'm sure it's because the concept of affirming my reality into existence was planted in me as a child, but I wasn't ready to take full ownership of that lesson. If she was right, then every negative thought I had risked drawing that negative thing into my life. I have no clue what was on my mind in those days, but I can only imagine it was at least partly composed of thoughts I did not want manifested. This was my first exposure to the law of attraction and clearly I wasn't ready for that level of personal responsibility.

Once I got to the airport, I did everything in my power to forget what I'd just heard. Then, a full six years later as I was leaving a venue in Baltimore, one of my students ran out and handed me a CD. She said, "Listen to this on the plane and bring it back to me next week."

I was in such a rush to get to the airport I threw it in my bag and drove off. Once above 10,000 feet, I got my huge plastic laptop out, plugged in my headphones, and inserted the CD into the drive. Clearly this was way before the days of iPhones and earbuds. Picture me relaxed in my seat on a peaceful flight excited to hear what my student was so anxious to share, and the first words I hear are a deep breath followed by a woman's voice saying good morning. As the audience chanted back good morning, I almost exploded out of my seat to get away.

It was the weight of the laptop on the damn seatback tray that kept me seated. I distinctly remember hitting pause and calling for the flight attendant. I was going to need a drink for this. Drink in hand, I took my own deep breath and hit play. As it turned out, this time I was ready.

Over those six years I'd discovered other authors like Gary Zukav who wrote *The Seat of the Soul* and Dr. Wayne Dyer's best seller *The Power of Intention.* It was their work that prepared me for Abraham-Hicks, so by the end of that flight, what started as a few notes ended up as a transcription of the whole speech more or less.

As my understanding of affirmations merged with my education in the law of attraction, I stopped freaking out so much about my own thoughts. Thankfully, what we think doesn't instantly appear in our lives. We are powerful manifesters, but we aren't instant manifesters. In place of fear and panic about my thoughts, I gained a broader awareness of what was going on between my ears. My thoughts were creating an internal story, and that story was being mirrored in my life. This of course happens for all of us, but still today most of the planet walks around either unaware or in stubborn denial of it.

Your Internal Story

You can't keep telling yourself the same story and expect a different outcome. Certainly you've noticed that when you are dwelling on a negative thought, you feel negativity in your body. Likewise, when you dwell on a positive thought, you feel good. This isn't groundbreaking, but have you considered that emotions are how the universe (God, source energy, whatever you might call it) communicates with us? Negative emotion isn't bad in and of itself. It's simply a tool the universe uses to let us know we're headed in the wrong direction. Sit with that thought for a minute because it can literally transform your life.

When you feel any negative emotion, it's life's way of trying to get your attention and let you know you're getting off track. Said another way, it means you're breaking your connection with source energy and letting a negative story spiral out of control in your mind. That's supposed to feel bad. Conversely, positive emotions are how the universe works to encourage us to keep going in that direction. Emotions are tools, but they aren't commands. It's important to remember you always have free agency to focus on whatever you want, positive or negative. The universe won't judge your choice, but it will follow your lead and bring you more of what you choose.

Here's how this plays out in daily life. We feel emotions when our brain has released a combination of various neurochemicals into our bodies in response to thoughts moving through our mind. This is why thoughts are things. Thoughts are very real and emotions are powerful drivers of action. Have you ever heard someone say, "She worried herself sick"? That's the perfect illustration of what I'm describing here. It's why you've seen so many people describe their version of the thought wheel. Thoughts lead to emotions; emotions lead to action; action produces a result; and any result, good or bad, triggers more thought.

We hear this described and then create cute sayings such as, "Doing the same thing over and over and expecting a different result is the definition of insanity." But that's not helpful. If you're even a casual observer of people (or yourself), you'll notice people don't usually vary that far from their patterns. Author and educator Dr. Joe Dispenza states that by age thirty-five a person is essentially a set of memorized patterns and behaviors. Jeez, what a depressing thought. So by age thirty-five, that's it? We're stuck? Thankfully not. Let's say I'm experiencing a result in my business I don't want, like not enough commission income. Conventional mindset training says just try to have different thoughts. But we all know it's not that easy. You have to work backward on the thought wheel.

If you want different results, remember that results come from action, so the first step to earning more commission is to change what you do—your actions. The only way to change what you are doing in any meaningful way is to change how you feel. You have to alter your emotional state because humans only do what they feel like doing, and you aren't an exception to that. Then, since thoughts are responsible for the emotions we feel, we have to change our thoughts and that's really challenging for many people. Here's why.

When you take an honest look at your life, you'll see patterns between the results you're getting in life and thoughts you typically carry around. You'll notice they correspond. That's because of the emotions and actions that rest between the two. And because we so easily get into patterns like Dr. Dispenza suggests, our stories become chronic.

If you happen to chronically tell yourself the story that salespeople are slimy, then you won't enjoy the commission income of a top producer. Conversely, if you chronically tell yourself the story that salespeople are servants in the marketplace doing important work, you're likely to thrive. This means, if you truly want to live the life of a top producer, you have to take control of the stories in your mind. You do that by controlling your inputs.

Where do thoughts come from and how do they even become chronic?

An input is anything that has your attention, and because you can direct your attention, you can create your own inputs. For example, playing with your dog or child is a great input that will trigger all kinds of pleasant thoughts, which in turn produce wonderful feeling emotions. And generally, any actions you take from that emotional state will be positive and productive. Inputs can also come from outside sources like mainstream media. If you start your day by watching stories about war, pandemics, and political fights, you shouldn't be surprised if your emotions are negative and your production is way off that day.

The more you become conscious of your inputs—news media being just one kind—the more control you'll have over your mindset and thus your career. But you'll only have that control if you remember that you are the only one who decides where your attention goes. In other words, if you take responsibility for where you place your attention, you get to live life around your priorities. If you let others go unchecked and feed you their inputs, you will be living life around their priorities.

This is why I'm a huge advocate for turning off all news because it makes us feel terrible within minutes. People who struggle to let go of the need to stay informed are essentially addicted to the drama. It's an easy addiction to understand because for survival's sake, humans evolved to prioritize the recognition of negative inputs. But these days we aren't under constant threat of attack by wild animals, and so the benefit of this prioritization has shifted. Rather than saving us from a bear, our need to stay informed saves us from rejection and from having to do critical business-building activities like lead generation. Think about this: how many people can you name who are legitimately living their best life while simultaneously paying attention to news media?

And speaking of our best life, the world is doing much better in many ways you rarely hear reported. Worldwide, people are being lifted out of extreme poverty faster than ever, and more people have food and shelter than ever before. If you can sit in air conditioning when it's hot and central heat when it's cold, you are living a life better than that of kings a century ago. What has changed is that the media have figured out how addictive it is to show us stories and images that produce outrage. So they do it often and on purpose, and we end up with the mistaken illusions that we need to stay informed because the world is going to hell in a handbasket.

None of this is supportive of your career. Or even your personal life. I mean, who wants to be around a person who is always depressed or angry at the world? Not your family, not your friends, and certainly not your clients.

As you can tell, I'm passionate about controlling inputs because most of them come along with someone else's agenda. Every call, text, and email you get is somebody who wants something from you, which may or may not be in alignment with what is actually important to you in the moment. But here's the thing: it's your mind and no one can enter it without your permission.

Because the vast majority of your competition walk around unconscious of what is happening, each day they suffer from exposure to any and every agenda but their own and can easily end the day totally drained but having accomplished nothing. This can be one of your advantages. A big key to living a Top Producer Life is keeping your head down and focusing on the life you want to manifest. You can ignore the rest. Really, if a society-changing event happens that you need to know about, you'll find out.

The Information Diet

If you're truly interested in controlling your inputs, start by going on an information diet. In much the same way a nutritional diet can snap your body back into a healthy state, an information diet can do the same for your business. The first step is to become conscious of all the inputs that surround your daily life and begin removing whatever is causing a problem. The easiest inputs to edit out of your life are television and radio news, including news-based podcasts.

If you've convinced yourself you are just staying informed, don't be surprised if you feel a bit of anxiety as you turn the channel and unsubscribe from the podcast. This feeling is temporary and normal, and you are on your way to much better feeling emotions.

Next, it's time to tackle your inbox. Any email lists you are on that don't make you feel good about yourself or the world need to go. For example, unsubscribe from all news emails, political campaigns, and stores that keep you in scarcity-based thinking by acting like this is the last big sale they'll ever have so you'll buy now.

Next, close the accounts for any services you don't use and delete any old digital content you've produced that isn't in alignment with who you are today. For me, that meant finding old blogs that I hadn't looked at in years and deleting them altogether. I was shocked at how many items were out there that would be better if just deleted. I found blog posts I'd written a decade earlier where I didn't even agree with myself anymore.

Finally, go through social media and unfriend and unfollow anyone (or any company) that doesn't make you feel good when you see their posts. If you have to debate it, they don't make you feel good so hit the unfriend button. I'll be honest with you. When I first did this, there was a huge group of people I easily unfollowed and unfriended. But eventually it got to a point where I was debating. I'd think, I kind of like this person, but we haven't communicated in any way in the last five years but— That's the same as saying, I used to like this dress, or this pair of shoes. I haven't worn them in the last five years but maybe they'll come back into fashion.

No. Just like you get rid of the shoes, delete the connection. Interestingly, after a few brave clicks of the unfriend button, it became fun, and I went from several thousand "friends" to under a hundred real friends and family. Then I decided to delete every Facebook post except for the last twelve months. I deleted my Twitter account altogether and started fresh with a new one. Instagram was even more interesting because it's so image based. If I saw an image that didn't make me feel good as I scrolled, I unfollowed the person immediately.

By the end of all of this, I realized this stuff was having a bigger effect on me than I'd realized. Because of the diet, I'd stopped comparing myself to everyone's highlight reels as much and began to see posts and images from people I really wanted to see. My email inbox was tamed and communication felt fast and efficient. It was as if my entire digital life had lightened up substantially. I suppose that's what any good diet does, right? Eliminate the fat.

There was something else I discovered the first time I eliminated so much junk from my digital life. I had more energy, an improved mood, and the ability to more easily place my focus on thoughts that supported living the life I desired. Of course, it's normal to stray from a healthy diet from time to time, and when you fall off the wagon, you can get right back on it by going on another information diet.

Using Adversity to Build Confidence

So you clean up your digital life and gain control over your inputs and life is perfect, right? Yeah right. Adversity is a part of life, and top producers understand it can be used to their advantage. No one really wants to experience adversity, but the least we can do is learn to use it to our advantage. The easiest way to do that is to reframe adversity as the way life attempts to bring us what we want.

A common early milestone in real estate is to close $2 million in sales volume in one year. Very often at that point, agents express the desire to double that to $4 million the next year. It's both a logical and exciting goal. Logical because at today's average home prices, $4 million shouldn't be a logistical nightmare and exciting because who wouldn't love to double their income?

The issue most people face is that they focus on the pleasure of twice the money and don't realize they just invited twice the number of problems into their lives. An agent who closes $2 million in volume in a year now knows how to handle all the problems that come along with that level of production. At one point, closing $2 million seemed hard but then it became easy. That's how growth works; hard becomes easy.

Then we experience a desire for more, for the next level, and we're back to hard, until that also becomes easy, and every new, bigger desire brings us back to hard. So when you state to the universe you want to double your production, you have to remember you just asked for two times as many problems. Initially that will feel like strong adversity, but the trick is not to wish it away. Those new adversities are life's attempt to deliver what you want. Life heard your request for double the production and is trying to give it to you. But first, you're going to have to learn to handle twice as many problems as before. Do that and your results will be right there waiting for you.

ADVERSITY + ACTION = CONFIDENCE

Once we've proven to ourselves we can do something, we no longer see it as a challenge and have built confidence to do it again because confidence is always obtained by taking action. There is simply no way to build your confidence first and then take action. This means as you grow, you'll learn that each new level you strive to attain will come with new adversities. At some point it will be totally obvious to you that all adversity is a tool. It's life's way of trying to give you what you said you wanted.

Ultimately, your ability to deal with adversity in your business, and life, comes down to the story in your head. As we've discussed, you can let the inputs of others dictate what that story will be and serve their agenda, or you can take responsibility for the inputs and get moving on your agenda.

The story in your head is made up of a series of thoughts. Studies show that the average human has about 60,000 thoughts per day, and 95 percent of those thoughts are repeated each day and 80 percent of our total thoughts tend to be negative. Yikes, no wonder this is such a huge topic. If the average human is having a series of repetitive negative thoughts, they have become a prisoner of their own minds, and this just won't do. In real estate you have no choice but to wake up each day and build momentum until you've reached a positive mental state.

It's so important to choose your own inputs because a belief is just a thought you keep thinking. It works like this: you have a thought, then the universe says yes and begins to deliver you evidence of your thought. When you notice it, you proclaim, see I was right and you have the same thought again, only this time it vibrates with more energy. Each time that happens, you build an even stronger belief.

When we trip upon a thought that resonates with us, but also contradicts a long-held belief, we call it cognitive dissonance. If you've ever been totally convinced of something only to have an experience that caused you to change your mind, then you've experienced cognitive dissonance, and you have firsthand knowledge of how beliefs are thoughts we keep thinking. Because of this new awareness, you started thinking a different thought regularly and changed your belief.

Once a person learns they can tell themselves a different story and develop a new belief, it becomes easier to do so on a topic like adversity. I think the most challenging part of this is that while we get to decide what we want, the universe decides how we get it.

Have you ever gone through a difficult period only to look back later and see clearly why events had to happen that way? This happens with many cancer patients. They didn't consciously ask to get cancer, but most people, when asked if they could go back in time, say they wouldn't change a thing. From their vantage point, it was clear why life delivered them the adversity of cancer and what they gained or learned because of it.

It wasn't until age thirty-five that I really started to understand this concept on a visceral level myself. I was going through a tough time professionally and was eventually able to work through the challenges. I remember the day I realized, once life had calmed down, that looking back at every struggle in my life, no matter how intense it had been, life always took care of me. That meant I could trust life was taking care of me now and will be taking care of me in the future—at every single moment. It was an incredibly comforting thought, so my question to you is, what will it take for you to let go of the struggle of adversity and acknowledge life is always taking care of you?

This is how you begin to connect the dots. You first acknowledge we live in an abundant and expanding universe, so when you express a desire for more—more clients, more money, or just more love and friendship—you're moving in the same direction as life. Life wants to expand and it's doing it through you. Each time you identify a new goal, which is just another expansion, in order to make that happen, life answers by delivering you new problems.

With a powerful mindset, you no longer try to avoid adversity and instead welcome it. I'm not saying it's going to feel great or be fun, but at least you'll understand what's going on and will be able to see it as the tool that you've been given. It's as if life is throwing you a test. It says, fix this problem and what you said you want is on the other side.

Most people do the exact opposite. They express desire for more and life responds accordingly by saying yes, fix this mess. Low producers see the mess and run away from it. Running away from it comes in many forms. There's resistance like complaining out loud or just in our minds, worry, stress, or at an extreme level despair, sadness, and depression. Some people even run away from problems by just stubbornly ignoring them.

The problem with running away from challenges in real estate is that if you express a desire to double your income and then resist all of the challenges that come along with it, life will hear that message too and begin to remove opportunities for growth.

Consider your identity as a top producer. Part of mastering the mindset macro is learning to maintain a healthy identity. When people enter the business of real estate, I generally find them to be well-rounded adults. They typically had a job that took up part of their life, and as I get to know them, I learn they are also identified as a mom or a dad, a best friend, and maybe a tennis player or a foodie. In part because of the comparison culture we're in, I've watched many people quickly narrow their identity exclusively to that of an agent. The parts of themselves they once enjoyed simply fade away.

At the start of a career in real estate this personality shift goes largely unnoticed by both the agent and their friends and family. When a person starts a new career and is seen as chasing after their dreams, they are usually supported. We like seeing people go for it because their efforts inspire us. The problem comes when the new agent isn't new anymore and has a more mature business but has let anyone and everyone cross their boundaries. When we don't hold our boundaries, it has the negative effect of destroying other important parts of our identities.

Too often, when an agent starts to earn commissions consistently, they realize they haven't seen their friends in way too long, they haven't been on the tennis court in forever and now resent their own business. Clearly, that's not a healthy mindset to maintain. Now, it's not like I can give you a list of five steps that will work universally for everyone to keep the real you from being lost in your profession, but we can cover some of the most effective ways that have worked for me and my clients over the years.

First, question everything. You don't have to run your practice exactly like everyone else does, even those you look up to. If the top producer in your office has his car wrapped with his face, logo, and website, and you don't want to do that, don't put pressure on yourself to do it. If you win an award for closing $10 million in volume and broadcasting that to the world doesn't feel right to you, don't do it. In fact, if selling only $5 million per year makes you happy, fantastic. Don't pressure yourself to do more just because awards are given to higher producers.

I've long thought the way we give out awards needs to change. I've seen quite a few $10 million producers who take home more money than $30 million producers who don't know how to build a team and manage their business. But on the surface, without further inquiry, everyone assumes the $30 million producer is doing better. And for that matter, think about a $5 million producer. That represents approximately $150,000 in gross commission revenue. With average home prices today, a $5 million producer shouldn't have a huge amount of overhead or out-of-control expenses.

How many Americans do you think would give their right arm for that amount of income? If you're making the money you want to make, hold your head high even if others seem to be celebrated. You can walk around proud that you are living your own version of the Top Producer Life.

A New Way to Look at Abundance and Money

Speaking of earnings, many people who get into real estate have a desire to dramatically increase their income but aren't aware of their limiting beliefs about money. It's stressful to wake up each day with a desire to thrive financially while simultaneously carrying the baggage of unaddressed fears around money. So because the Top Producer Life comes with plenty of financial resources, we need to strengthen your mindset around the topic of money.

Southwest Airlines may allow you to carry on two bags for free, but I'm asking you to put your baggage down. Top Producer Life Airlines has a no money baggage whatsoever policy.

Can you finish any of these sentences?

- ▶ Money is the root of all _____. (I know the full sentence is "The love of money" but you still finished it didn't you?)
- ▶ You can't take it _____ _____.
- ▶ Money doesn't grow on _____.
- ▶ The rich get richer and the poor get _____.

The fact that we all can finish those sentences and even add to the list indicates we have limiting beliefs around money, and those beliefs will make it really hard to live your Top Producer Life. We can't believe we live in an abundant universe and also believe any of those statements. The two competing mindsets must be resolved.

In my experience it doesn't really matter if you grew up around a lot of money or if your family barely scraped by. People with great wealth can be just as limited by a fear of losing what they've amassed. The place to start is to acknowledge that no matter what you observed as you grew up, you have the right to develop your own thoughts about money, and you definitely have the right to be wealthy.

If you're a spiritual person, consider a universe with unlimited abundance. If you're more religious, go to Matthew 25:14 and read the parable of the talents. If you have a scientific mind, remember that everything in the universe is energy, including money, that can't be created or destroyed. It's merely transformed and always there for us as an inexhaustible resource. In all three cases (spiritual, religious, and scientific), we end up in the same place, so it's to your advantage to set your mind to the fact you have the ability to generate all the money you desire. The only person who can stop you is you.

This way of thinking has always been easy for me, and I believe it's because I was exposed to Zig Ziglar at such an early age. His most famous saying is, "You can get anything out of life that you want as long as you first help enough other people get what they want." Once I built some momentum in my sales career, I began to see that I could literally have anything I wanted.

If I wanted a new car and it cost $50,000, all I had to do was look at my average commission. If it was $5,000 then all I needed to do was help ten extra families above the baseline number I needed to help to cover my living expenses. Help a defined number of people, buy the thing. To me that thought was so empowering and so fun it has been a huge driving force behind each step in my own career.

Some people hide from their money out of shame or virtue signaling while others flash their material possessions in an attempt to boost their self-esteem. But you don't have to do either because living an authentic Top Producer Life means you understand that material possessions and experiences you buy with money are symbols. Specifically, they are symbolic of the people you've most recently helped. In other words, if you didn't help someone first, you wouldn't have the money to spend.

When you think about money this way, you free yourself from guilt and are positioned to do really great work in the world that goes way beyond helping just yourself. If you want a Porsche 911 and a Rolex, go help enough people and they're yours. And if you want to help fund a school for children in a third-world country or set up a college scholarship fund, help some more people with their real estate and then go spread goodwill throughout the world. But remember, you can't do any of that if you hang on to limiting beliefs about money.

Real estate has a way of making everyone think they have to be a local celebrity, and agents tend to compare themselves to each other relentlessly. It's one of the only professions I can think of not listed on a stock exchange that broadcasts earnings on business cards.

Think about how much easier it might be to maintain a healthy mindset around money if we stopped shouting from the rooftop how many millions we've sold and instead put all of our focus on the number of families we've helped. In my opinion the world is headed in that direction anyway. People want to feel as if they are being listened to and that you intimately understand their situation. Agents (and coaches for that matter) who talk endlessly about themselves and their awards are only pushing people away. Those who are willing to shine the light on their clients first are the ones who will lead the way.

PLAYING TO WIN

Once you start to get a healthy mindset around money, it becomes easier to play to win. Most people don't play to win, they play not to lose and I can prove it. Do you think you'd work harder to earn $2,000 or harder to keep someone from stealing $2,000 from you? If you're normal, you'd work harder to keep someone from stealing from you. That doesn't automatically make you a person who plays not to lose, it's just a good way to illustrate the difference.

When we play not to lose, we are firmly within a scarcity-based mindset. People who play not to lose often ride the production and income roller coaster in real estate and eventually hit a plateau. Often people who want to be a $10 million producer will get stuck around $6 million. This isn't because they lack the skill, it's because at $6 million they have enough extra money to put some away and unconsciously begin working to keep it. In other words, if a person has an extra $10,000 in the bank after all other expenses are covered, it's easy to get stuck guarding against losing it. Spending energy trying to protect savings is an example of playing not to lose.

Alternatively, playing to win means you push yourself into uncomfortable territory even if that comes with a risk of failure. I remember when a student of mine named Rachel negotiated her first above-average listing commission of 8 percent. Initially she had doubts anyone would pay her a commission that high, but after our coaching sessions, she committed to give it a shot and try some of the negotiating techniques I taught her.

Most salespeople are so worried about losing a listing, they won't even allow themselves to try new strategies. Acting to protect the possibility of losing a listing that you don't even have yet is definitely playing not to lose. Rachel wanted to play to win.

Soon after she landed the high commission, she went on a listing appointment and did one of the hardest things a salesperson can do: she closed three times. When she asked for a signature on her listing agreement, the seller hesitated. That was close number one and most agents stop here. They don't want to be seen as pushy, and, because of that, they leave and let the seller think about it. This is another example of playing not to lose and, ironically, causes most agents to lose the business anyway.

Rachel fought back her nerves, continued the conversation, and then closed a second time. Guess what? The seller hesitated and gave her another objection. What would you do in this scenario? Would you have the guts to ask for the signature one more time? You would, but only if you were playing to win. I can imagine Rachel freaking out inside, but she took a deep breath, asked a few more questions, and then closed for the third time.

You already know I wouldn't be writing this story if the seller didn't sign. They did and Rachel went home that evening with a new $565,000 listing and a potential $16,950 commission. And if you're wondering, I'll teach you how to close three times in the next section. For now, remember, when you're living a Top Producer Life, it means you're playing to win.

You're the Boss: This Is How to Act Like It

So far, we've discussed mindset from a general point of view, and now we need to look at two specific states of mind that top producers learn to move between on a daily basis. The first is the mindset of a boss, and the second is that of an employee. One is not better than the other, but you can't survive with only one.

In corporate America, someone has to own the role of the boss, and others must own the role of employee. Together they make the business thrive; but if a company loses all their employees, they risk going out of business. Likewise, if there is no leader, the company falls into chaos. When you choose to be self-employed, you have to learn to be both boss and employee each day.

You're not the boss of me. I'm told as a child I had a fiercely independent attitude and frequently got in trouble for screaming that line at authority figures. So I suppose it makes sense I've always been self-employed. After years of observing thousands of my students struggle to control their schedule, I realized no one really teaches agents how to be an effective boss. There are plenty of leadership books out there, but most people in real estate aren't leading large organizations. So what about leading yourself?

When people talk about designing the perfect daily schedule, they're getting close, but what's really needed is a broader and more complete understanding of what it means to lead yourself as a self-employed business owner. This goes beyond trying to force yourself into a rigid daily schedule. The good boss mindset is a way of thinking that sets you up to live the life of a top producer. Specifically, it includes

- ▶ Your Big Why + Your Goals
- ▶ The Weekly Preview
- ▶ Quarterly Personal Retreat

YOUR BIG WHY + YOUR GOALS

Your goals and the reasons you are in real estate are intimately linked, so to live the life of a top producer, you'll need to spend significant time thinking about them, just like the boss of any large company would. Odds are, the real reasons you got into real estate aren't about money but about the specific lifestyle you imagine yourself living. That lifestyle will take a certain amount of money, but money itself isn't the goal.

One of the easiest ways to gain clarity on your big why is to project your thinking into the future, assume you're living the life you've dreamed, and write about it. Grab a journal and allow yourself the time to get it out of your head and onto paper. This is a critical step in manifesting your vision. For some people the vision will be paying off all debt, and for others it'll be buying enough of their own real estate to generate cash flow that will support them in retirement.

As you write, ask yourself why is what I just wrote important to me. As you keep asking that question, you will eventually get to a place where you're deeply connected to your core motivations. You know you've gone deep enough when you look at what you've written and feel the emotion behind it. When you're at that point, it's time to visualize your work by adding imagery. That could be a vision board, a picture on your desk, screen saver and smartphone wallpaper, or a tangible object that reminds you of why you really got into real estate.

There's no wrong way to do this. Just remember, your big why has to be important enough to you that the thought of not achieving it is worse than any other problem you could encounter building your business. It has to be important enough that rejection, failure, losing a client, or the temporary frustration of struggling while learning new skills are all minor in comparison to not achieving your vision.

A top producer doesn't spend time sweating the small stuff. Anytime you find yourself stressing over day-to-day inconveniences that come along with being self-employed, you know you have narrowed your focus to the small stuff. This is when it's time to lift your head up and think bigger. The visual you create is what you turn to in order to reestablish your focus on your big why.

For example, if what you want more than anything is to be able to travel the world without worrying about money, an image of your favorite city on your phone lock screen can be a fantastic way to stay connected to that vision. When you find yourself stressed about your business, that symbol will help you snap out of it and stay on track. Thinking bigger is always the fastest way to escape frustration and negativity.

Your big why will change as you grow and accomplish more in your career. The best part about maintaining clarity is that goal setting becomes easy when you have it. While average agents struggle year after year with their goals, top producers simply ask one question: Will achieving this goal get me closer to living out my vision? If the answer is yes, they go for it.

When I was first licensed, my big why was to prove I could be successful in life without a college degree. That was important to me because it was drilled into my head as a kid that a college degree was the only way to make it in the world, but I hated college. I would face anything in business if it meant I didn't have to sit in a boring classroom. Just thinking about it evoked strong emotion.

So my first two goals were to sell enough to cover my monthly living expenses and to buy a new car. I went to a dealership and got a brochure of the car I wanted and kept it with me at all times. I even had a coach convince me to attach a laminated, 8 x 11 picture of the car to my keychain! Every time I saw the picture, I was reminded of my big why, and being able to pay my bills and buy the car clearly got me closer to my vision. Obviously, life moved on and my goals got bigger and the same will happen to you.

Identifying your big why and establishing goals that support it doesn't have to be that complicated. You just need to allow yourself the time to work through it and remember to change up your goals as you grow. If you do that, business can always be fresh and exciting.

THE WEEKLY PREVIEW:

HOW TOP PRODUCERS CONTROL THEIR SCHEDULE

Most people spend too much time doing their work and not enough time thinking about their work. In corporate America, it's easy to get away with this because you have a boss who does much of the thinking for you. But when you're self-employed, you have to take the time regularly to think about your business. That's what it means to work "on" your business as opposed to "in" it.

Specifically, you'll need regularly scheduled times when you can lock out the world and think from the mindset of a boss. Over time you'll develop a process that works for you. To get you started I'm going to describe my own. It's called the Weekly Preview. The goal is not simply to reflect on what you've done (review), but to decide what you'll do next (pre-view). To be the most effective, establish a regular time block for your weekly preview. (Mine is Friday from 9:00 a.m. to noon), then go through these steps.

1. Review your wins: Write out what you're most proud of accomplishing during the week.
2. Review your action: Write out what worked well and what didn't. Most importantly, give yourself permission to stop doing tasks that didn't advance you closer to your goals.
3. Clear your inboxes, voice mail, text messages, and DMs: Go through your email inbox and ruthlessly delete messages you don't need. Respond to those emails you may have forgotten or put off and archive the rest. Do the same with your text messages and DMs.
4. Clear your notes and to-do lists: Go through any notes and to-do lists you maintain to catch what's still important and trash what's not needed.
5. Establish the big three goals for next week: Based on what you've just reviewed, think about what you want to accomplish next week. What three tasks, if done, will get you closer to your goals?
6. Time block the next week: Now that you've decided what is important, transfer the individual tasks you need to do to your calendar using time blocks.

When you commit to a weekly preview, you'll finish the week before you even start it, and you'll never walk into work on Monday wondering what you need to do. You'll also have a major head start on your competition each and every week.

QUARTERLY PERSONAL RETREAT:
HOW TO TAKE A REAL, GUILT-FREE VACATION

For most people, the word *vacation* evokes an extended period of time where you can disconnect, not just from your business, but from your day-to-day life. If you went to work for a company, part of your benefits package would include a certain number of vacation days. When I was in high school, my dad worked for a semiconductor company that gave employees a sabbatical every seven years.

After he gave seven years of his life to the company, he'd get a month of paid time off. I remember how excited he'd get as that time approached and how he'd talk excitedly about what he'd do with the time. When his sabbatical arrived, he'd built it up so big in his mind that it was never going to live up to what he dreamed.

There was something about my father's experience that felt wrong for me. I never spoke to him about it, but I remember thinking I'd never want to give a company so much control over my life. Maybe that's one of the reasons I left college and got my license at eighteen. There must have been a part of my subconscious mind driving me away from that kind of professional life.

Clearly, you don't want that life either. Working for yourself means no one is going to tell you when to take vacation. You will never have a client say to you, "I see how hard you've been working and think you need some time off." So if no one is going to give you time off for a vacation, you are going to have to take it.

Instead of the pressure of a vacation, my partner, Jon, and

I go on quarterly retreats. Both of us are self-employed and have found that if we go away for the typical vacation, by the time we finally disconnect from the patterns of day-to-day life, there's only a little time left to truly enjoy the vacation. That alone created more stress as we anticipated the energy required to get back into the swing of things at home. It's almost as if the vacation was counterproductive.

Have you ever taken a trip only to feel like you need a vacation from your vacation? That happened to us, too, and the quarterly personal retreat was our solution. Here's how it works: each quarter we go somewhere we enjoy and stay for at least a week, but usually longer. We don't even try to slip into what most people think of as vacation mode, meaning we still get up early and go through our morning routines. I still get my workout done, I still set intentions for the day, and I still get myself into a positive mindset. After we've both finished our morning routines, we sit down and work.

On the retreat we work together and talk about what is going on in our businesses. We talk about the projects that are working and those that are not. He gives me his input on my projects, and I'll do the same for his projects. We don't have a formal structure for this process and that's a deliberate choice we made. One day we might talk exclusively about my business and other days we may focus entirely on his.

The goal is to help each other and to make sure that what we are doing individually is adding up to the life we say we want to live together. Having these deep discussions at regular intervals keeps us in alignment and from getting too far off track. It allows the space for us to make changes if needed and to learn about how we are growing. It's also important for the health of the relationship.

Sometimes after our discussion we'll actually do some work on individual tasks. Picture the two of us sitting at a table with our laptops and journals spread out working on whatever the discussion has inspired us to do. This only goes on for the first half of the day, until roughly noon. Then we put work away and go do all the typical activities people do on vacation. It's a type of retreat that works well for us, and these days we plan our retreats a year in advance because, just like you, no one is going to walk up to us and instruct us to take some time away from daily life. We leave all that behind when we enter the world of self-employment.

The great advantage of a retreat is the benefits are there even if your family doesn't look like mine. You might have kids, or a spouse with a corporate job (or no job), or maybe you're single and your family is your friends. In any case, you can take the spirit of the quarterly retreat and deliberately build your future no matter how many people live under your roof.

Mastering self-leadership is only half of the equation. Like I discussed earlier, every company needs good employees and that means if it's just you, you have to learn how to perform for yourself like you would for any other boss. In other words, be the model employee. Or at the very least try not to get fired.

The good employee mindset comes with its own way of thinking that empowers you to take consistent actions in support of your ultimate vision. When combined with the good boss mindset, you'll be operating effectively and in a way that propels you to your Top Producer Life. Specifically, a good employee

- ▶ Starts each day with intention
- ▶ Lives the done-by-noon lifestyle
- ▶ Ends each day deliberately (evening routine)

Live the Done-by-Noon Lifestyle and Outproduce Everyone in Record Time

To be productive, you can't just wake up every day and go into the world reacting to what happens around you. Our industry, and I suppose every industry, is full of people who start their day by hopping on email. Doing that ensures a long day of reacting to the world with little to no production to show for it.

Starting the day with intention means you do what you need to do to get into a positive mental state, ready to take action. To do this you need a morning ritual. There is no perfect way to do a ritual, so there is no point in trying to copy someone else's perfect daily schedule. One of the secrets to success is to take control of your day from the very beginning in a way that works for you. That means it's your responsibility to design a process that is easy to maintain.

My own process looks like this: I wake up and immediately jump out of bed to throw on my gym clothes, which were laid out the night before. I don't allow any time to lie around in bed because the point is to raise my energy, not hit the snooze button and lower it. For me, exercise is a form of meditation, and rather than listen to music while working out, I listen to speakers like Abraham-Hicks, Dr. Wayne Dyer, and Joel Osteen, to name a few.

After an hour of listening to their messages while moving my body, I feel like I can conquer the world. Then I use a free app called the 5 Minute Journal to express gratitude, state my overall intention for the day, and write out an affirmation. I intermittently fast daily, which means I don't eat breakfast. Instead, I feed my dog, Chug, and take him out for a brisk walk. After that I make the bed, shower, get dressed for the day, and head into my office. I've timed my routine many times, and it always comes in about three hours.

Use my routine as a model to design your own but, before you do, notice a few strategies. I don't consume news of any kind in the morning, and I don't open emails, text messages, or social media apps. There is little if anything positive to be found in any of that, and at some point you will have to make the decision that your agenda matters most. Living the life of a top producer means you absolutely cannot afford to let other people's agendas drive your actions, especially at the beginning of the day.

Routines and schedules are important, but even those who strongly advocate for a perfect daily schedule rarely follow one themselves. In any case, there is a much easier way to remain super productive and that's to commit to the done-by-noon lifestyle.

Have you noticed how at some point during the day, your smartphone goes into power save mode? When that happens, it's trying to conserve energy so the battery lasts as long as possible and does so by slowing down functions that suck up the battery. We all know what it's like being tethered to a charger if we wait too long to plug in and the battery hits the red zone.

You are powered by energy just like your smartphone. From the moment you get out of bed, everything you do and everything that gets even a tiny bit of your attention requires energy. And just like your smartphone, at some point you're going to need to be plugged in for a recharge. But humans can't plug into a socket. We can take naps, but the very best charge we get each day comes overnight as we sleep. By noon, most of us hit power save mode, at least mentally.

Modern life encourages us to power through the day and the problem with that is we aren't using our full power for most of it. Would you want a surgeon to operate on you when he was fully charged in the morning or in the afternoon when he downed a few espressos because he was on power save mode?

Early in my career, I noticed almost every top producer recognized the importance of controlling their morning. One of the most memorable examples was a single mom in my office named Kelly. My desk was near hers and she'd always be there working already as I strolled into the office casually with my venti mocha frappuccino. She always got to the office by 7:30 or 8:00 a.m. and would work on her mindset as she built momentum in her day.

Then, at exactly 9:00 a.m., she'd grab her leads box and pick up the phone to make her lead generation calls for no less than one hour. In those days, everyone had recipe card boxes with 1–31 dividers in them representing the days in the month. Each lead we got went on a card and we'd put the card behind the day we intended to follow up. Kelly was so consistent in her lead generation that she had four boxes on her desk. At the time, all of my leads for an entire month fit into one box. I figured if I ever wanted four boxes of leads, I'd better pay closer attention to what she did.

I learned that because she had a son in school and no spouse to back her up, she had no choice but to get her most important work done before noon. After that, she was going to have to get her appointments done and pick up her son or he'd be left standing outside in the school yard. Kelly wasn't thinking about her day in terms of being a good boss and employee, she was thinking about being a good mom.

You may not be a single mom, but you certainly have other parts of your life that will suffer if you don't perform well at work. So the done-by-noon lifestyle at its core is a philosophy that you must take control of your day and do your most important work by noon when you are most likely in a state of peak performance. That doesn't mean you stop work at noon, but it means if you chose to stop midday, you'd still be out-producing everyone around you. And anyone living the Top Producer Life knows that when you do your most important work by noon, you often can't stop work for the day because then you have to go see the clients and prospects who need you.

For most people, the idea of a done-by-noon lifestyle is exciting, until they realize it means they'll be ignoring external inputs for the first half of the day and then they panic. What I mean is, unless it's a true emergency, you'll have to ignore calls, text messages, emails, and everything else coming at you in favor of doing your most important work, which is outgoing in nature. For example, prospecting is critical for your business, and you can't do that on a high level if you aren't focused. Chronic low producers have an unconscious habit of not controlling their morning because it gives them an excuse not to prospect. So to help you avoid feelings of panic or guilt, let's look at a few more ways of thinking to support your Top Producer Life.

The Workday Shutdown: How to Keep Your Career from Taking over Your Life

When people think of time blocking, they usually imagine a start and end time on the calendar for a business event or task. To accomplish your biggest goals, you'll need to begin thinking of everything in your life as an appointment, which likely sounds restrictive. But the freedom self-employed people seek over their schedule comes from a bit of structure. The idea is to tightly control your day until noon, then allow for flexibility the remainder of the day.

Throughout the entire day, whatever you choose to do is thought of (and gets recorded as) an appointment. You deserve all the benefits that come along with being self-employed and that includes being able to go to the gym or shopping any time you want. But to enjoy those benefits, you must understand how much time you actually have in a day.

One day has a mere 1,440 minutes and you really don't have much time to waste. Think about the last time someone asked if you had a minute. Did it take exactly 60 seconds to hear them out? It likely took much more than that, especially if they were in a bad mood and needed to get something off their chest. Let's pretend you chat with them for 20 minutes. That doesn't sound so bad at first, but studies show it takes 25 minutes to get refocused on what you were doing before any interruption. That's a total of 45 minutes out of your day for the person who asked if you had just one minute.

Now think this through. How many times do you need to be interrupted before you end the day emotionally drained and stressed because you know you weren't particularly productive? The answer is not that many. The issue gets worse when you consider our digital distractions. Literally every feature on your smartphone is designed to capture and keep your attention. If you want to learn how to run your day, not only do you have to think of everything as an appointment, you've got to take responsibility for your own minutes. What that really means is you have to own the interruptions by realizing no person or thing is interrupting you. But by allowing people or devices to capture your attention, you are interrupting yourself.

Here are some additional ways to regain control of your daily minutes and prevent interruptions.

▶ Turn off all notifications on your smartphone, tablets, laptops, and smartwatches. On my personal phone there are only three apps allowed to display notifications on the screen. The first is the phone app because the only way to stop the phone from ringing when a call comes in is to go into airplane mode. The second is my calendar app. This is safe because I control my calendar. If I'm alerted to an upcoming appointment, it's because I chose to be alerted. And the third is called MyShake because I live in California and would like a few seconds heads-up if the big one hits. I only allow the red notification bubble on apps so, for example, I can see how many text messages I have, but to read the messages I have to open the app. And there's even debate over whether we should allow that because the color red is designed to get our attention.

▶ Move all of your apps over one screen. This way, when you unlock your phone you see a totally black screen except the apps at the bottom. The half second it takes to swipe left for the rest of your apps is almost always enough to help you put the phone back down when you've grabbed it out of habit or boredom.

▶ Use a 1440 sign. The visual reminder will help you stay focused when you are in an environment prone to interruptions. When someone walks up to you and asks if you have a minute, look at the sign, then look at them and say, "I'd love to help, but can't right now." Then smile and turn back to what you were working on. At first this might seem harsh, especially if you love being the one to help. Ask yourself, why are you so eager to help? When you allow the interruption, what are you getting to avoid? It's so easy to point the blame at all the distractions until we realize that by allowing them, we usually benefit by getting to avoid something that makes us uncomfortable.

To a large degree, being a good employee these days can be seen as the act of minimizing distractions so you have the energy and mental bandwidth to get the most important tasks done each day. Thinking like a good boss has gotten you out of bed, in the right mindset, and rocketed you into the day. Thinking like a good employee ensures the important work gets done by noon and remembering that every single distraction that has our attention drains the battery.

END EACH DAY DELIBERATELY

Real estate careers develop in predictable patterns. First, it's critical to build in structure and build up momentum. From there it takes about two years of having your head down working on the basics. As you steadily increase your production, new problems will surface and the biggest of those will be time. The busier you get, the more important it becomes to be mindful of how you handle the end of the day. Having a full roster of clients is wonderful until they become resented.

If you're brand new, this might not make sense initially. Why would anyone resent their clients? In truth, no one does intentionally, but the resentment sneaks in through the back door as an agent with no control over their day gets busier. I know it's happened when I hear this: "My phone rings all day, I can't keep up with email, and my spouse gets angry with me because I always have to take calls at dinner and on the weekend. I'm worried because I'm starting to resent my clients."

I don't know many companies that would be cool with their employees hanging around the office every night and every weekend. Maybe occasionally to meet a deadline but not every day. Often agents think being self-employed means they have to be available 24/7 or their entire practice will come crashing down. Let that sink in for a minute. People want to work for themselves in order to control their own schedule only to reach a point where they have given up complete control.

Picture this scenario: It's Saturday and you're headed to a kite festival with the family. On the way, your phone rings and it's a client. You look at your spouse who's driving and you get "that look." In the nicest voice you can muster, you promise it will only be a minute. Then you answer the phone because, well, because you have lost all sense of boundaries. Two hours later, that one call has turned into four more and honey is waving to you because the kids are done and it's time to go eat.

You've missed the whole event. And for what? To be a superagent and give your life away because you think that equals good customer service? Because being available 24/7 is required or you won't make any money? Well, Nordstrom delivers legendary customer service and I can't reach their employees after hours. And guess who sets those hours? Not me. Nordstrom does. I don't think they are awful people, and I don't stop doing business with them because they close in the evening or because my preferred salesperson has regular days off. Heck, Chick-fil-A thrives in part because they so publicly close when their competition doesn't.

This is how people begin to resent their career and it's damaging to personal relationships and clients. Your clients need you at your best, which means you need time away from your business to refresh. You need time for your mind to wander in order to come up with creative solutions for transactions and inspiration for marketing to attract fresh leads. You need time to be a complete human and not just an agent. After all, the point of business is to fund your life, not define and control it.

To prevent this from happening, or to correct an out-of-control situation, you must decide when work stops each night. It doesn't have to be the exact same time each night, but a decision must be made each day. To help you transition into your personal life, you need an evening routine that does the opposite of the morning routine. The morning routine powers up your day; the evening routine powers it down. You only need about thirty minutes to accomplish this transition. So if you are going to stop work at 6:00 p.m., here's what you do at 5:30:

▶ Check email, DMs, and voice mail one last time for emergencies and respond to truly urgent requests.
▶ Review and acknowledge what you did well that day.
▶ Review and acknowledge what didn't go so well. What could you have done better?
▶ Review your calendar for the next day. Decide your three most important tasks for the next day and time block them, before noon if possible.

Then go home. No more work. It's time to be a good mom, dad, wife, husband, partner, friend. But what if there is an offer to negotiate? Okay, what if there is? You likely knew it was in the works and this is a perfect example of the need to set boundaries. If you decided work ends at 6:00 p.m. so you can go to your son's game, then everyone involved should be put on notice. If it's urgent to a client, let them know it needs to get done by 6:00 because, after that, you're unavailable. No further explanation needed.

I know this sounds unrealistic to many reading this right now. So remember, I'm writing not only from my own years of experience selling real estate but from the experience guiding thousands of other agents on this very issue. People only think it's unrealistic because they've accepted the story that everyone else's agenda is more important than their own. Once you change the story in your own mind, you learn people quickly change with you. What once seemed impossible becomes, "Oh, why didn't I do this in the first place?"

Remember, when a decision is made, it needs to be communicated. If you decide you generally stop work at 6:00 each day, that expectation needs to be set at the listing appointment or buyer's consultation so your clients understand your boundaries. You may have to gently remind them from time to time, but that's as simple as saying, "I have other commitments starting at six this evening. What do we need to do to get this done before then or would tomorrow be okay?" Part of holding your boundaries when working for yourself means you aren't under any obligation to explain your other commitments.

One more thought about boundaries. What if you cross them yourself?

I mean, what if you go home but can't stay present because you're thinking about work or, worse, don't put down your smartphone? Well, when it comes to the smartphone, I'm not an addiction specialist so all I can tell you is that at some point you have to decide humans are more important than the phone and put it in the other room or just turn it off. But when it comes to your thoughts and turning off your mind, a journal would be really helpful.

Even with the smartphone turned off, you are going to have thoughts about work when you go home. And if you only had one thought, it would be okay but about every seven minutes you're going to have another thought about what you need to do tomorrow.

Low producers try to remember everything and then wonder why they can't shut their mind off when they go to bed. Top producers have a trusted place to record all these thoughts. Imagine cooking dinner and having a great conversation with the family. When a work thought pops into your head, you pause the conversation, record the thought in the journal, then resume, giving your full attention to the conversation. Do that as many times a night as needed. Your loved ones will actually feel loved, and you won't forget anything the next morning.

YOUR DAY OFF

While we're on the topic of letting go of work each night, we need to address regular time off. Occasionally, I'll run across an ad being run by an agent who advertises being available 24/7. They are trying to communicate that they are dedicated and available to their clients, but saying they're available 24/7 is the easy way out and it's also a lie. Everyone knows better so why even say it?

I've never hired anyone because they were available around the clock. In fact, the opposite is true. When I go to the dentist, ideally I want them to have just returned from a vacation relaxed and centered. And when my CPA does my taxes, I really hope they have been taking time off to recharge before working on my file. There is a joke that if you need business when you're an agent, just schedule a trip and prospects will come out of the woodwork.

In my observation, too many people in our profession never schedule time away for fear of missing out on a commission. It's a clear manifestation of scarcity-based thinking. The irony is that if you walk around worried about missing a deal when you step away from your business, you'll become so burned out that you will begin making all kinds of mistakes and miss lots of business. Worrying is using our imagination to manifest what we don't want.

I get it, being self-employed is intense, and in the beginning you will have a stronger desire than you ever will again to realize your vision. But especially at the beginning, you face a choice. Learn how to take care of yourself now or spend thousands of dollars in coaching learning how to do so when you are juggling ten clients at a time. Obviously, it's going to be easier to learn this now.

While corporate America thinks of their regular time off as the weekend, you get to choose whatever you want. I never watched *Downton Abbey* but I do have a favorite scene that's become popular on YouTube. Over a meal, someone references the weekend, and Maggie Smith's character, a countess, with complete sincerity asks, "What's a weekend?" It's the perfect question to be asked by someone who doesn't work for a living.

Of course a countess would have no concept of a weekend or of even needing time off. Time off from what? Being a countess? But since you're an agent and not a countess, I'm guessing you'd like some time away even if your marketing suggests otherwise.

Just because the majority of the world is programmed to think of the weekend as their time off doesn't mean you have to. Like many of you, I didn't just snap my fingers and fix my scarcity-based thinking. When I started, I was afraid of taking time off too. So I decided I'd pick one day and for a reason I no longer remember, Sunday was it. In those days we used paper calendars, and my coach encouraged me to mark off Sunday with a thick black marker.

I was warned that as soon as I decided Sunday was my day off I'd be tested and, sure enough, Friday afternoon before my very first scheduled day off, the relocation department called me to say the buyers I'd worked with for weeks decided at the last minute to fly in and they were ready to buy. Talk about a challenge. I remember my coach saying, "Jasen, one deal more or less will not make or break you, but the inability to take care of yourself and hold your boundaries will drive you out of the business long term."

In effect, she was asking me to think about the big picture and reframed the choice I was about to make. Was I going to hold my boundary by taking my day off and find an alternate solution or would I give in and take the client out to show property? The first choice allowed me to hold my own power and would benefit me long term. The second choice may have provided instant relief, but it would come at the expense of teaching myself, and everyone else in my life, that I wasn't worth any time off and that I had to exist at the whim of everyone's agenda but my own.

I have worked with so many people who struggled over this exact issue, but on that day I made the choice to take my day off. My coach didn't tell me what to do; she merely asked the question and made sure I'd own my decision. I asked an agent in the office who didn't have much going on to help me out. If he would show the homes on Sunday, I'd pay him a fee for his time. It worked perfectly and that was the beginning of an entire career of Sundays off that continues to this day.

Imagine for a minute what kind of support you'd get from your family if, on your day off, they see your phone blowing up and you completely ignore it, remaining present with them. Do that and not only will you be demonstrating wonderful life skills for your children, you'll be supported on the rare days when you need an exception. Although by then you won't want the exception even if they'd be cool with it.

Of all three business macros, mindset is the most important. Everything else in your career can be going well, but if you skip the work necessary to balance this macro, eventually you'll run into trouble. You could make tons of money, but it would come at the expense of your mental health, personal relationships and interests, and your family life.

You've no doubt noticed there is a ton of information about controlling your time in this chapter. When you fail to set your mind properly, the first structural system that falls apart in your business is your calendar. You suffer because you've given away your power and move through your days based on other people's agendas instead of your own. And of course no matter how skilled a salesperson you become, you'll never realize the fullest version of your Top Producer Life by operating on the agendas of others.

Over time, you'll find that as you apply the material in the next two chapters, you'll encounter opportunities to revisit this section and learn the concepts on a deeper level. When you push yourself to grow, you'll naturally stray from the patterns you've put in place. When that happens, don't beat yourself up. Nothing is wrong. It means you are growing and the solution is to come back to this chapter and start reading. You'll find new levels of understanding that weren't available to you this time through. When the student is ready, the teacher appears.

5

▼

Sales Methodologies: The Tools of Top Producers

I've asked some of my most devoted students over the years to finish this sentence: "When you get good at selling—" and some of the common responses are you can earn unlimited income, you have control over your future, and, my favorite, you have superpowers.

Getting good at selling to me is exactly like having superpowers because people tend to feel that way. Even if you don't always use the word *superpower*, it means you have learned how to take control of your activities and your income and you are clear on how you will serve people in order to live the lifestyle you've always dreamed of living.

Obviously you could have chosen tons of industries, but you picked real estate, and your sales methodologies are how you are going to build whatever you want from here on out. I should warn you, though, getting good at selling is highly addictive.

You may not sell real estate for the rest of your life, but once you have developed yourself as a salesperson, you'll likely always view yourself as one wherever you go professionally.

One of my favorite sayings is that when you learn to sell "something," you can sell "anything." As you grow, you'll start to see signs of this ability all around you that go far beyond business. Being able to sell anything means you can persuade your spouse or partner to do what they might normally resist. You'll be able to persuade your children and friends to take action. You'll be able to raise money for charities you enjoy supporting, and you'll even be able to persuade people to do you favors such as making space for you in a crowded restaurant or giving you the upgrade you could really use when traveling.

Serving at a high level as a salesperson will bring a lot of power into your life and business. Salesmanship is leading a person to a place where they feel safe doing what they wanted to do in the first place. When I start teaching people the various methodologies of a top producer, there is a tendency to resist for fear of being seen as pushy.

If you ever feel as if you're being pushy or if it seems you're being viewed that way, the reason is almost always because your intent is not in alignment with the client. Understanding this is the difference between fearlessly using your skills to serve another human and enjoying a richly rewarding career and constantly worrying about how you're being seen.

Ironically, those who resist learning salesmanship are most likely to put pressure on their client and come off as pushy. When you can't sell, your income drops. When your income drops, you panic and try to force situations. In this way, you become the very thing you so badly wanted to avoid. The saddest part is that this is often unconscious behavior.

At the end of the day, it doesn't matter how persuasive you become; you're still never going to be able to make someone do what they don't want to do. Unless you carry a gun around on your appointments, no one is going to do what they don't feel like doing. Conversely, humans always do what they feel like doing even if they are working with the world's worst salesperson.

In this context, you should feel totally free and unrestrained in the use of any sales skill you obtain. If you use it and it works, the results mean you made the client feel safe moving forward with what they wanted. That's an amazing feat to be able to do for another human being. Combine this with an intent to think about the client first at all times and you simply can't go wrong. You won't be seen as a pushy salesperson. Instead, you'll be thanked for your professional persistence.

In this chapter we're going to build your sales skills in three steps. First, we're going to talk about lead generation and building your database, because there's no point in learning how to sell if you don't have any clients. Second, we'll work through the various methodologies you'll use to take a listing lead from initial inquiry to the listing appointment. Third, we'll work on corresponding methodologies that take a buyer from inquiry to signed buyer agreement to a submitted offer.

We save buyers for last because top producers operate with a listing-first intention. Learning to build a listing inventory gives you direct control over your income in the same way inventory drives any other industry. Whoever has the product to sell is always able to make money. It's as simple as that. Building and managing a listing inventory is a little more complicated than working with buyers, so don't feel bad if your business is heavily weighted with buyers. If you're newer or if no one ever taught you how to master listings, that's to be expected. In either case, set your intention now to think listing first.

One last point: If you're a buyer's agent on a team, don't skip the sections on listings. One day you might want to start a team of your own, and even if not, learning about listings will improve your performance with buyers in lots of intangible ways.

Lead Generation: Your Only Real Job

Before you sprint out into the world striking up lots of conversations, let's look at your primary business asset, your book of business, which is to say the tangible asset you have created that comprises the data generated from your interactions with other humans. This is not a sphere of influence. Everyone has one of those but not many have a real book of business.

For context, a five-year-old has a sphere of influence. It's her friends on the playground, but of course she doesn't have a business. Likewise, your competition also has a sphere of influence, but most of them have not done the work necessary to formalize their spheres of influence into a book of business. To do that, you need to choose a customer relationship management (CRM) system.

Odds are your company has one, and if not, just perform a Google search on "CRM for real estate" and you'll be able to check out whatever latest and greatest options are out there. The goal is to find one that has most of the features you think you'll need and is priced within your budget. Don't overanalyze your options and get stuck with paralysis by analysis. You will never find the perfect CRM, so identify one that does most of what you need, and if a better one comes along in the future, you can always export data from one and import it into another.

Once you have your CRM system, it's time to import the data you already have by pulling together the various spheres of influence in your own life. This task is likely to be in direct opposition to what you'd like to be doing. People who get into sales rarely want to sit at a laptop and screw around with a CRM all day. But what if I told you that this one task could put you light-years ahead of your competition?

Start by making a list of all of the places you have information on other people. That would be your smartphone, your email accounts (all of them, even the old ones you haven't logged into forever), your social media accounts, and even old paper files. What about neighborhood rosters or church group directories? If you've been in the business for a while, find all your old leads, open house rosters, and files from closed transactions. Keep building this list until you're confident you've identified all the places you are connected to other people and their contact information.

Then, import those people to your CRM. Even if all you have is a name and email address, that's fine. Also, if you've been in the business for a while, what about all the people who bought your listings? Add them too. Odds are you'll do a better job staying in relationship with them than their previous agent.

Once you've added everyone to one central system, you should notice a couple things: first you probably know a lot more people than you realized, and, second, you most certainly have huge holes in your database. For example, you have a name and a mobile number but no email address or vice versa. This is normal, so filling the holes will be one of your hidden advantages in the marketplace. It might surprise you to learn just how many agents in every market are flying by the seat of their pants saying a silent prayer that the economy holds up and they are able to maintain momentum. They never take the time to record all the wonderful data they have about the people they know and have worked for. It's all just swimming in their head.

This is a problem because you can't do much with it unless you can recall all the data on command Erin Brockovich–style. And at the end of your career, you won't be able to sell your practice or pass it on in some way. Have you ever gotten that letter from your dentist that they are moving and introducing you to your new dentist? Well, your old dentist sold you. Okay not you, but the information your dentist built up on you and their relationship with you over time. That has real value and is sold regularly in other industries.

That same opportunity exists in real estate, but usually only brokers do it. Interestingly, agents have all the power to do this because the public rarely has a relationship with the company and broker. That is the domain of the individual agent.

So because you can sell your data later on and because much of your competition is frankly too lazy to maintain a proper book of business, you are sitting right in front of a massive opportunity.

Once everyone is centralized, you only need to make a simple commitment to fill in the holes in the data over time. Every time you communicate with someone, you have a chance to fill holes and add more layers of data. When I say data, there is the obvious name, phone number, email, physical address, and so on. But those are the basics. The real power comes from all of those often overlooked details like birthdays, pet names, pet birthdays, kids' birthdays, hobbies, anniversaries, funny stories about the last time you worked together, details about their careers and their ambitions, and favorite foods.

The more of this information you have at your fingertips, the better, and these days you can even cheat a little by noting what you learn about people on social media. The key is to get in the habit of capturing all of it in your CRM.

Your book of business is your business.

THE RELATIONSHIP GAME

Not everyone in your book of business has equal value. Although that may sound cold at first, you probably have a great relationship with at least one company that has put you into a group. Do you travel a lot? If so, you likely have your favorite travel companies, and they definitely have you in a group. They even tell you which group by giving you status. For a good fifteen-year period, I traveled on Southwest Airlines multiple times a week. In those days, I was worth way more to the airline than the average passenger. If there was one seat left on a flight, and we both wanted it, you would have been out of luck.

I'm not suggesting you publicly issue a status to people in your book of business, although that's an interesting thought, but everyone in your system should have two classifications that you can reference. Some systems call them tags, others call them categories, but at a minimum you need to know the source of the relationship and its status. The source is simply how you came into contact with a person. That could be networking, an open house, a personal referral, or some event. The quality of your relationship is its status and, like on social media, is fluid and can change from time to time. To determine relationship status, you play the relationship game.

Imagine a huge pyramid in the middle of the desert. This is the most amazing pyramid you have ever seen. As you see it in your mind's eye, you instinctively know it's a structure to be treasured and protected. There is a small door at the bottom, and as you walk through, you see a huge ground floor with massive amounts of square footage. You also notice an amazing staircase. As you look up, you can see it leads to three more floors above you. Then you notice a velvet rope and security on the staircase before each floor giving you the sense that people can't just walk up to the top floor.

Each higher floor has a smaller amount of square footage, so you gather that making your way past each velvet rope to a higher floor has some meaning and significance. You begin to wonder how one gets to the top, and that's when you see me walking toward you. We sit down and I explain to you that this amazing structure is yours and was built for you the day you decided to get your license.

Just like a pharaoh's pyramid is prepared from birth, yours was prepared at the birth of your real estate dream. However, instead of sitting there waiting for your eventual death, this pyramid represents the opposite. This one is for the life of your business. It was built as a home for all of the people in the marketplace you will connect with and serve.

As you take ownership of this massive piece of real estate and begin filling it with the people you know, you realize you're going to have to make some decisions on where people are allowed to go. You can't have people running all over the place inside your pyramid. That would be chaotic and stressful on everyone. Plus, if you ever needed to find someone, it could take forever. So you decide you need some rules.

To keep track of people coming into your pyramid, you put

a nametag on them and two wristbands—one indicating they have access to the ground floor and another indicating how you met them. Before they get access to more intimate parts of your pyramid, you need to get to know them a little better. So while they are on the ground floor, you communicate with them at regular intervals until the day you notice they start to engage with you and express interest in what you do. When that happens, you lead them to the staircase and instruct security to let them past the velvet rope so they can check out the second floor. Before they walk up, you take the wristband for the ground floor off and give them one that allows access to the second floor.

When you visit your guests on this floor, you are able to accelerate the speed at which you build your relationship, and because of this, many of these people turn to you when they need help. This comes in two forms: either they have a direct and personal need for your service or they want to connect you with someone who does. When this happens, you recognize the significance of the relationship, because when one human puts their trust in another for the first time, they are sticking their neck out and taking a chance.

To reward their trust, you again lead them to the staircase and invite them through the next velvet rope to explore the third floor, which is smaller still. Of course, before they walk up, you remove the second-floor wristband and give them one that allows third-floor access.

On the third floor something amazing happens. People here begin to form a community around a common experience—in this case, working with you. They see proof that you have served others well and that you honor and respect them by treating them differently than all the people roaming around downstairs.

Once they notice they are being given special treatment, they naturally want more of it, so they continue with the behavior that got them to this floor. That usually means they connect you with more people they feel you can help. At that point, you walk them to the last velvet rope, give them the VIP wristband, and invite them to the fourth floor at the top of your pyramid. This is the penthouse and is the smallest but most luxurious floor. It's where all the best your house has to offer is located. People here feel so special that anytime they leave the pyramid they can't help but talk about you and regularly connect you with new people to serve. No one wants their VIP wristband removed.

Okay so let's come back out of the fantasy world for a minute. How did that feel? Would you like to have a pyramid like that? The good news is that the relationship game is a mental exercise you play with yourself. The components of the pyramid correlate to parts of your book of business.

Think of the pyramid itself as your CRM system. The CRM is going to hold all of the people who come into contact with you from any source. When you first connect with someone, and enter them into your CRM, it's as if they have walked through the door of your pyramid and this is where you tag them with the source of contact. Most real estate CRM platforms will have source categories preinstalled such as personal referral, open house, or sign call. It doesn't matter what categories you use as long as they make sense to you and that everyone has one when they go into your system. That's the one wristband that stays on them for the life of your business.

You only meet someone for the first time once, and at some point you will want to know where you tend to connect with the most people. Without these tags or categories, you'll be forced to guess.

The next wristband or tag/category you put on people changes depending on their behavior. I've found people have the most success with a lettering system and use it myself. If you were to look at your name in my CRM, you'd see a minimum of two tags. Maybe you have the book tag because we first were connected when you bought this book. And the second would be a letter indicating the status of our relationship. There are only four letters that correspond with the floors in the pyramid. The bottom floor is labeled C, the second floor is B, the third floor is A, and the fourth floor or the penthouse is A+.

The C label is for people you've connected with and for whom there is potential to do business. If you think about that, it doesn't take much to get a C wristband and gain access to the bottom floor. You want that barrier to entry to be low so you can get as many people into your pyramid as possible.

The B label is reserved for people who have started to respond to you. They are beginning to demonstrate that they see you as a real estate agent and this comes in various forms. Maybe they ask you a question about the market, respond to your email newsletter, or comment on your Instagram post about real estate. All of that and more are signs that the status of your relationship is improving. When you recognize any behavior like this, bump up their status in your CRM. It's important to pay just a little bit more attention to your Bs and critical to maintain consistency with whatever you've done to nurture them to this point. At any moment they could choose to take the most important action they ever could for your business—send a referral. The moment they do that, bump their status.

The A label is reserved for people who have referred someone to you for help with real estate. This includes people who hire you for their own needs because, essentially, when someone does that, they have referred themselves. Getting people from the C group to the A group is how you win the relationship game. You can't survive in real estate without enough As, and because it takes time and effort to get people to that point, you might as well make a game of it and allow yourself to enjoy the process. As you deepen your relationship with your A list (thank you Southwest Airlines), you will find you have some especially enthusiastic supporters.

The A+ label is reserved for your fans. That's the best way to describe your biggest supporters. Even if you feel like in the beginning your only real fan is Grandma, don't sweat it. Remember, the penthouse doesn't have room for a ton of people anyway, and the qualification to gain access should be high. A fan is someone who trusts you so much that they send you multiple referrals a year without you even asking. They are literally your advocates in the marketplace on a daily basis.

To put this into perspective, after thirteen years of selling homes in Austin, I only had thirty-two A+s in my book of business. Doesn't sound like that many does it? However, that meant each day I had thirty-two people in my town who were like little referral antennas. Every time there was someone in their orbit who needed to buy or sell, they went out of their way to connect us.

Estimating conservatively, that group sent an average of two referrals per person each year for a total of sixty-four referrals. So let's say I sucked at conversion and could only convert around 30 percent of those referrals. That would translate to about twenty transactions that at an average sales price of

$350,000 would equal $7 million in production. Seven million in production handed to you, in addition to business you generate from the other levels of your pyramid. Sounds like a game worth playing doesn't it?

To be sure, you are an A+ for at least one other professional, and although they likely don't think of it this way, you should be starting to understand that the concept plays out in nearly all industries. Is there a stylist, a dog sitter, or even a brand for which you strongly advocate? If so, you are an A+ for them. Playing the relationship game allows you to become deliberate about nurturing people instead of letting your business develop by accident.

REFERRAL SECRETS OF TOP PRODUCERS

Referrals are often misunderstood. Most people think when they receive a referral, the sender of that referral is trying to help them. While there may be some truth to that, the primary reason people send referrals is to make themselves look good. The act of sending a referral is an unconscious attempt to improve social standing.

If someone sends you a referral and you do a great job, the sender's social status with the client you helped is enhanced. Conversely, if the transaction doesn't go well, that status is diminished. This is why it's so important to cultivate your relationships in a way that makes people feel it's safe to refer you. Fear of loss is a much greater motivator than opportunity to gain. If there's any reason to doubt your performance, people would rather not risk their reputation. The fascinating part of all of this is that it mostly goes unsaid. So to generate the referrals you deserve, learn the referral secrets of top producers.

Rule 1: You have to ask.

"Who do you know who is thinking of selling or buying a home in the near future?" That question or your variant is possibly the most important question in your entire career, and you cannot shy away from it. People love to help other people, but they can't read your mind. If you never ask for referrals, you'll end up giving the impression that you don't need any more business. But I've never met an agent for whom that was true, so open up and give people the chance to help you.

Rule 2: Demonstrate the actions of an agent.

You told people you got your license and now they'll forever remember to refer you, right? Not so fast. Whatever you spent years doing just before is how they think of you, especially in the beginning of your career. If you were a teacher before you got into real estate, in their mind, you're still a teacher. The single most impactful action you can take to change the way they see you is to demonstrate you're doing the activities an agent does—and not just listings and closings. Think property tours, classes, open houses, and industry events.

Show people you are actively involved in your new industry and tell stories about your experiences growing your business. Slowly but surely people will start to take you seriously. But in the beginning of your career, or anytime you've been inconsistent, they won't see you as a serious agent.

Rule 3: Teach people when to send you referrals.

Handing people your card and asking them to pass it to someone thinking of moving won't cut it. Instead, consider asking them to save your cards for people who experience a life-changing event. For example: "Here's my card. Please save it for someone who is going through a big change. Give it to someone who tells you they just got a promotion or that they are having a baby." Or you could tell people to mention you when they hear people are getting married, divorced, had a death in the family, sent the last kid off to college, or complain about all the yard work or their commute. You get the point.

Change (good and bad) drives the need for your services. Over time, you can teach people in your book of business to recognize these triggering events so they are more likely to connect you.

Rule 4: Tell people what you do, not what you are.

The last time someone asked what you do, did you tell them you're a real estate agent? When people ask what we do, most answer with what we are. Professionally you are an agent, but as an agent, what you do is help people when they experience change. Adjusting the way you answer could elicit some funny responses, and you'll be simultaneously teaching them how to refer you. Imagine someone asking what you do, and instead of saying you're an agent, you say, "I work with people who are getting divorced." Very likely the person who asked will respond with, "Oh, you're an attorney?" To which you can respond, "Oh, no. I'm a real estate agent and I help divorcing couples sell their home without strangling each other."

Now that's just one of an almost endless number of ways for you to use this referral rule. The key is to respond in a way that is both unique to your personality and a tad more memorable than telling them you're an agent.

Rule 5: Frequent and consistent contact is essential.
In marketing the rule of seven states that a person needs to see your message an average of seven times before they take action. Most people who suffer from a lack of referrals do so not because of the exact number of messages they send, but because their messages are irregular and don't register with the recipient.

You'll find lots of opinions about what you should send people, how often you should call, and what you should say. The truth is that no answer is right because they are all right. Pick whatever combination of marketing and pattern of delivery you want, but whatever you choose, it must be consistent and frequent because in the subconscious mind, consistency equals trust.

Agents who send messages at random, when they can fit it in their schedule or when they have extra money for the marketing campaign, often don't even realize they are broadcasting they are either broke or can't handle their own business. Because all of this registers in the subconscious mind, people in your book of business aren't literally thinking you can't handle your business. Rather, they are always thinking of themselves, and to protect themselves, if they don't trust you, you'll never be referred. This is why communication of any kind that is poorly designed but consistent wins every time over the stunningly beautiful but inconsistent email newsletter.

Rule 6: Don't stop.
This rule is a bit repetitive and that's intentional because it's so important. You can't stop until you retire or sell your practice. You can't stop asking. You can't stop teaching people how to refer you. You can't stop showing them you are an active agent.

Apple consistently advertises the iPhone, and if you notice, they also haven't stopped. The most successful and recognized consumer device in the history of the world is still being consistently advertised. If Apple can't stop, neither can you.

Rule 7: Remember they are taking a chance on you.

Every time someone sends you a referral, they are putting their reputation on the line. This is especially true the first time. So if you want them to continue to send you referrals, you must always keep this top of mind. It's not too difficult to get people to take a chance on you once, but if you don't act in a way that enhances their reputation, you may not get another. The key word is *enhance*.

It's not enough to do a good job for the client. That's kind of like saying you should do a good job as a parent. For most parents I know, a good job is the baseline. What they really want is to be a great parent and enhance the lives of their children. To encourage more referrals from the same source, you have to find ways to serve the client so well, the reputation of the person making the referral is actually improved because of your performance.

One of the best ways to do this is to speak highly of the referral source to the referred client. In addition to doing a great job for the buyer or seller, sneak in a few complimentary comments about your referral source. You can be sure that, eventually, your new client is going to tell your referral source all the nice things you've been saying. Psychologically, this is infinitely more impactful than just giving the compliment to the source in person.

Rule 8: Reward the referral, not the closing.

Whether we're talking about children, pets, or clients, it helps your cause to reward the behavior you want to continue. It's a common practice for agents to send a thank you gift to referral sources after closing. But when people refer you, they have no control over whether a deal closes or not. Or if the referral even turns into a deal in the first place. People can control making the connection and that's it. Sometimes it works out, sometimes not. If you want to send a gift after closing, fine. Just make sure you thank them in some tangible way immediately after they send the referral.

Rule 9: Communicate more than you are inclined.

It would be a huge mistake (and a missed opportunity to strengthen the relationship) to accept a referral, then fail to let the source know what's going on. Clearly, it's important to keep the details of your client's business private, so think of it this way: every few weeks you can send the referral source a message letting them know the work is progressing and you're on it. Even if things have stalled out, it's important to say so. If the referral source ever wonders what's happening, you've waited too long and have probably broken trust.

My standard was to update all clients and referral sources once a week, even if it's a quick email or text message. That was enough to prevent anyone from ever wondering what was going on. It was also consistent, which reinforced trust.

Rule 10: Don't be afraid to decline a referral.

You don't have to work every referral sent to you. But you definitely should communicate with the referral source when and why you decline business. Remember, the goal is to make the source look great, and if you can't, don't want to, or aren't truly qualified to work the referral, it's okay to let them know. This is your chance to show appreciation while reinforcing the message that you'll only take on business if doing so will enhance their reputation. The end result is more clarity for them on the type of business you enjoy working. Most people power through working business they shouldn't because they fear turning it down will prevent the source from referring anyone else.

In reality, the exact opposite is true. When you work business you don't want just because you feel like you have to, everyone is going to feel it. It may go unsaid, but under those conditions, it's nearly impossible to do your best work for the client, let alone put in the extra effort to make your referral source look good.

Rule 11: Share good reviews with your referral source.
One way to get future business from those who are researching you online is to ask for five-star reviews on Google and Facebook. Another way to leverage good reviews is to call attention to them with the source of the referral. A handwritten note with the review printed or an email with a screen shot is a great way to reinforce that you've made the person who sent the referral look fantastic.

Rule 12: Reciprocate.
Does your referral source also own a business? Are they a partner (or trying to make partner) at a firm? Ask what kinds of referrals they would like back and stay super-alert for opportunities to send business their way. Of course, you're sticking your neck out as well so be mindful of their performance. Does

their performance with your referral enhance your reputation? This process works both ways.

WHAT TO DO IF YOU'RE NEW OR HAVE NO MONEY

Referrals are ideal, but what if you're new to real estate or new to your area? When I was a new agent, I'd attend seminars where top producing agents were on panels. When asked how they got their business, the most common answer was "all my business is repeat and referral business."

Well, wonderful, but that didn't help much when I was eighteen, new to business, and had no money. I knew a ton of people in my city, but the problem was that they were also eighteen and most were just starting college. I could ask my connections who they knew that was thinking of buying or selling (which I did) and unless the answer was "my mom or dad," even that magical question wasn't going to pay off in any meaningful way for a while.

So if this new career was going to work for me, I had to connect with a bunch of new people and fast. When I work with someone who is new to a city and has chosen real estate as their career, I can absolutely relate. Even though I knew a ton of people, I might as well have just moved when I started. Functionally it was the same experience.

If you're in this position, the first point I want to make is that your status is temporary. The second is that it's time to hustle. Until you have enough money to support yourself, you won't have the ability to invest in a meaningful and consistent way in your marketing. When you're in hustle mode, everything is on the table regarding lead generation. That means you need to be doing open houses, talking to people in your book of business, striking up conversations with strangers, knocking on doors, and even calling strangers. No lead and no opportunity to talk to someone new should be passed up.

THE HOMELESS BUYER METHOD

When you do talk to people, in addition to asking generally who they know that is thinking of moving or, specifically, who has experienced a life-changing event like a promotion, you can use the homeless buyer method. This method of prospecting focuses on caring for consumers in a way that most other human beings would want to be cared for if they were in the market.

The idea is that either you or an agent in your firm is working with a buyer who has not found a home, and under that premise, your prospecting is aimed at finding people who would consider selling. This method works in person, in print or digital, and on the phone; just be sure you follow your broker's do not call policy when using the phone.

To get started all you need is basic information on a buyer currently in the market who's still looking. It could be your buyer or one represented by another agent at your company, just don't make them up. When you approach potential sellers, start by asking if they'd thought of selling. You'll almost always hear no, but instead of letting that stop you, tell them the only reason you ask is to help find a home for your company's homeless buyer. Give them a few basic details about the buyer and why they want to live in that area, then ask again if the homeowner has considered selling. You might still get a no, but at the very least, you've left a great impression on the person as a hard worker. But often, you'll uncover seller leads that others would walk right on by.

LAST CALL BEST CALL

Blocking out an hour of time for active prospecting is the most important action you can ever take for the health of your business, and while most of your competition will forever resist it, you can actually make it fun. You know those crazy people (like me) who love going to the gym every day? You can be the crazy agent who loves your prospecting hour every day. If you think about it, all you have to do is start conversations with people and get them to talk about themselves or describe how you're working to help another family. In both cases you're simply being a good human being. And sometime before the end of the conversation, ask for what you want—a connection to someone who is thinking of moving.

One more item I want to address is how you finish each prospecting session. When you are prospecting, the last call is almost always the best call. Every time you reach the end of your scheduled prospecting time, you'll face a choice: Move on, which if you have another appointment you may need to do, or keep going until you have one more conversation. One last call that could be your best call.

When I lead workshops we even turn that into our mantra—last call best call. Let's pretend that three times per week you have a few extra minutes to squeeze out one more conversation. That would be 156 extra conversations over the course of the year. And let's say that just 10 percent of those lead to any business. That's fifteen extra sales. Take a minute and quantify that. What is your average sales price? That's how many more millions of dollars in production? As you can see, it's a powerful methodology for sales.

Scheduling Appointments:
Convince People to Enthusiastically Meet with You

THE CONVERSION CHAIN

What if I told you that most agents don't need more leads? Don't get me wrong, more leads are always nice, but the truth is, you'll benefit tremendously by learning to lose fewer leads.

When average producers come across a new lead, if it doesn't convert immediately, they just move on to the next one. Top producers, however, use a method to capture and nurture their leads so it's far less likely they'll lose them. The method is called the conversion chain, and it goes beyond a simple follow-up plan for leads.

The conversion chain is a systematic way to guide leads from initial inquiry to the initial appointment. Once you learn it, a couple significant changes are going to occur. First, you'll never wonder what your next move should be with any lead you generate, and because of that, you'll lose fewer. Second, because you'll know how to get people to schedule time with you, your confidence when prospecting will skyrocket. To be sure, this skill is critical to building your Top Producer Life because of all of the time and energy you'll put into generating leads in the first place.

The conversion chain has four parts, and it works because it provides the space necessary for your prospect to travel the mental journey needed to agree to an in-person meeting with you. Sometimes it helps to look at what not to do. When your average competitor runs across a hot lead, in a fit of excited panic, they essentially jump down the prospect's throat and ask for an appointment. If it's a seller lead they run across, the next sentence out of their mouth is something like, "Let me come over and show you what I can do."

Are you old enough to remember the show *MADtv* and the man-baby character Stuart? If not, stop now and do a Google search for, "Stuart, look what I can do." After you wipe your eyes from tears of laughter, imagine this as your competition. The truth is, no seller is going to be inspired to give you an appointment to "see what you can do."

The four parts of the conversion chain are text, talk, table, and terms, and you can think of them as individual links. Your ability to consistently live the life of a top producer will only be as strong as your weakest link, so let's examine each link.

Text: Very often, communication starts with a lead via some sort of text-based conversation. You either get an email or a text or DM on social inquiring about a property or other real estate–related issue.

Talk: This link is all about the phone. When the lead starts communicating with you digitally in some form, your first goal is to get them on the phone so you can talk to them. Leads can come in initially on the phone as well, such as when you get a sign call on a listing, and in that case you simply focus on the next link.

Table: This link is all about the appointment. Once you have a person on the phone, your only goal is to get them to agree to an in-person appointment.

Terms: The final link is about the terms of the agreement with your new client. This is best accomplished in person as you get your representation agreement signed.

One Step at a Time

As you can see, the links move from one to the other and provide a framework so you always know what to do next. Rather than getting overly excited and blurting out your version of "look what I can do," you can simply focus on the next link in the chain. Moving people from one link to the next requires three separate conversions (unless they start by calling you, in which case you'd only need two conversions).

This method works well because it allows both parties to take it one step at a time. I'm sure you've experienced a time when you spoke with someone on the phone and thought they were going to be wonderful clients, but when you met them, you realized what they wanted was not even remotely possible in your current market. If that hasn't happened to you yet, it will soon enough. Eventually we learn that we don't want to work with everyone, and using the conversion chain slows the process just enough for you to take control and make your evaluation.

SALES MAGNETS

To move people through the links in the chain you'll need tools. I call them sales magnets. They can be used three ways: to generate leads, to schedule appointments, and to obtain signatures. A sales magnet is simply an idea, reduced to a visual, given a name, and used to persuade people. Think about the comparative market analysis or CMA. Why do you use a CMA on a listing appointment? Because you are trying to educate the seller on the market? Well, yes, but on a more basic level have you considered why?

When you first got into the business, you learned about market analysis in school, then observed everyone in your office using them. But have you ever thought to ask why the people you observed do CMAs? It's because when they first got into the business they saw other people doing them and followed along. We could go back generation after generation and we'd see people using CMAs because they think they have to. I'm not suggesting you shouldn't use CMAs. Some brokers require them even when working with buyers. I'm asking you to think about how we got to a place where everyone accepts this as routine business.

I don't know who it was or where they were, but if you could get a time machine and go back into history, you'd eventually find the very first agent who used a market analysis to compare properties. But I'd bet they didn't call it a CMA then. This was likely an agent who was looking for a way to attract (like a magnet, get it?) new business. I'm sure they thought: *Hmm, I know what those ranches sold for. And I know what those people want for their ranch over there. So maybe if I shared this with the other ranch owner who is considering selling, they'd hire me to sell theirs.*

And you know what? It must have worked. It had to have worked because I'm sure at some point this agent, whoever it was, decided to write down the information and then give it a title. Who even knows if it was initially called a comparative market analysis? All we know for sure is that by the time you and I came along, it was already a long-established business practice and had matured to a point where software programs generate them for us.

But when you strip away the software and get right down to it, the humble CMA was probably the industry's first sales magnet. To this day, it's used to persuade people to take action. If you can think in this way about sales magnets, you are only limited by your imagination. Literally anything you can think of could be used to create a sales magnet, and once you have it, you get to choose whether to use it to generate leads, schedule appointments, or persuade someone to sign an agreement. A CMA will certainly work well for all three and, for that matter, you could even extract components of the CMA to create new sales magnets.

For example, do you ever run across potential sellers who are more concerned about time than money? Well here's an example of how you can take the idea of using market timing data from a CMA and create an entirely new tool.

Consider what eats up time when selling a home beyond the average days sitting on the market. First you have preparation and staging time. Then you have average days on the market, but what about off-market sales? Those data are missing. And how do you account for expired listings? If I listed a home and it expired after 180 days, then you listed it and sold it in 14 days, the sold record will report 14 days. But the house actually took 194 days to sell.

When you take over the listing, even though my 180 days may be reflected somewhere, average days on market is calculated using sold listings only, tracked by listing number. In this case, since my listing is expired and not sold, my 180 days aren't included. It's an inherent flaw in every Multiple Listing Service (MLS) I've ever seen, so smart agents will use this to their advantage.

One way to adjust is to take the average days on market shown by the MLS and add on half of that number to account for off-market listing and those that expired before they sold. It's not scientific, but it doesn't need to be. The whole point is to prepare the seller with an idea of how long it will really take to bank their equity. And because MLS systems stop the time when a property is marked pending, we also need to prepare the seller for processing time.

As you can see, for a seller who is more interested in timing, you can persuade them to meet you by offering a more robust explanation than average days on market in a CMA. To make it a usable sales magnet, all you have to do is take this idea, make them visual, and give the visual a name. In workshops I've led in the past, agents have chosen to call this a real estate market timer. But that's what they chose, and you have the freedom to come up with your own name.

While we're on that topic, you could also rename the CMA. There's no law that says you have to call it a comparative market analysis. Here's an idea I've often used in the field. Take the concept of the CMA, expand the search to a few adjacent neighborhoods, and remove the pending and sold data. Then you have a set of homes more like what a buyer would consider checking out before making an offer. Especially in a strong seller's market, that view of the market will help them make sure they are asking the highest possible price, wouldn't it?

After all, a CMA looks backward in time with heavily weighted sold data, and this new approach helps you project forward by looking at what new sellers are attempting to get. What could you call a tool like this? A maximum market price forecaster? Call it what you want, that's the whole point.

Now that you have a working knowledge of the conversion chain and what a sales magnet is, you simply need to learn how to make the three conversions. When you understand that, you'll be on your way to an award-winning career as a top producer. It's not an understatement to say that you can screw up a lot of stuff, but if you master this skill, you'll still be unstoppable.

HOW TO GO FROM TEXT TO TALK

There is a concept called the 7 percent rule that comes from a book called *Silent Messages* by Albert Mehrabian published in 1971. In the book, the author combined the results from two different studies on communication and concluded that 7 percent of our communication is verbal and 93 percent is nonverbal with the nonverbal part being composed of our tone of voice and body language.

Our tone of voice, he states, is responsible for another 38 percent of our ability to communicate and the remaining 55 percent comes from our body language. Over the years his ideas have been both championed by well-intentioned speakers and torn apart by researchers who argue with his science. The only important question is whether you can use any of this information to your advantage.

To see that you can, think of the last time you read an email and got upset only to learn later that you totally misinterpreted the intent of the sender. Because you assumed the wrong tone, you got stressed over nothing. So while researchers argue over science and percentages of communication, a top producer understands they are able to convey their message with more clarity and persuasion if they are using 100 percent of their means of communication (words, tone of voice, and body language) regardless of percentages.

Somehow we have convinced ourselves that no one wants to talk on the phone anymore. My guess is that agents see their children texting constantly, even joking about people who still make calls, then they make the mistaken conclusion that no one wants to talk on the phone.

When I was a kid, it was common for parents to become frustrated when their kids tied up the phone line for hours.

The modern equivalent is children spending hours staring at a screen texting. There's no doubt that digital communication is faster and more efficient for routine messages. We make the mistake when we fail to realize that when the topic of conversation is important or complicated, we are wired as humans to crave a more connected way to communicate.

For example, I may trade text messages with my CPA about routine issues, but when this issue is more complex like how should I adjust my strategy based on these tax law changes, all of a sudden I want to hear his voice, and I may even want to discuss in person. Your prospects are no different. It's fine to communicate via text message when all they want is routine information about a listing. But the second they become serious about moving, their instincts will drive them to seek deeper connection.

HOW TO NURTURE TEXT-BASED LEADS

When you understand that consumers will talk to you when they become serious about moving, nurturing leads becomes a simple function of maintaining a connection and keeping the conversation going. For example, when you get a message with a question on a listing, your responses should be designed in a way that both provides information to them and to you. Think of it as trading information. First they ask a question about the listing, then you answer and now it's your turn. You get to ask a return question and that's an important key because one of the basic tenets of selling is the one who is asking questions is the one who is in control.

The fastest way to get good at asking return questions is to develop an honest curiosity about people. You can do that by activating your inner five-year-old. You know the one who asks Mom a question and after her answer the child asks why? No matter what the next answer is, the mom finds herself being peppered with an endless string of whys. This is the energy I want you to conjure up when you're working with leads.

You know how the tech industry says information wants to be free? Okay well, in real estate it basically is. Most of the questions you get about a house are already answered online, and if the prospect looked hard enough, they'd find it (such as number of bedrooms, square footage, annual property tax, school district). So when they ask you for these types of details, they're really asking for a shortcut.

I suspect you don't like working for free so how do you get paid for saving them the time to look it up themselves? Your payment comes in the form of information about them. Somewhere within this text chain of trading information, you'll want to attempt the first conversion to a phone call. The sooner you can find your opening to suggest a call, the better.

A few years ago I wanted to demonstrate this for a group of agents I was coaching in person. We were in the office, and I asked them to let me know when the next inquiry came in online. It wasn't long before someone sent a message through the company Facebook page expressing interest in looking at homes to rent.

I took over the keyboard and guided the lead through the conversion track. We traded eight messages total before the first conversion to the phone was made, four from her and four from me. On my fourth message I suggested a phone call and her fourth message agreed and included her phone number. First conversion, check. (Check out the following screenshots for the exact conversation.)

Recent studies tell us you have the best chance of converting an incoming lead by responding within two minutes. Not long ago it was quoted as five minutes. Another statistic shows you still have a good chance of converting if you respond within an hour or so. In my mind, it doesn't matter whether it's best to respond in an hour or two minutes. You can't build a career you enjoy while feeling as if you have to monitor your incoming messages every few minutes, and you certainly don't want to walk around worried you're missing out on a lead.

Conversely, it would be a mistake to ignore leads or treat them with a cavalier attitude. Every inquiry you get represents a combination of your time, money, and energy spent, and I know you don't want to waste that.

Today we have technology that will allow chat bots to take over and engage the lead when you can't, but someone has to tell the chatbot what to say. Human or bot, we still have to follow the conversion chain. In all cases,

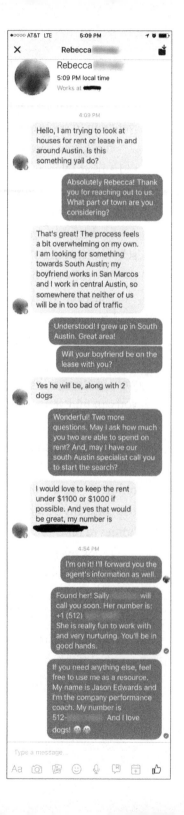

when a lead comes in from any source, the first goal is to slow them down if you hope to have any chance of converting them.

Consumers want you to respond as fast as possible, but that doesn't mean they won't slow down if you engage them and capture their attention. Have you ever been in a rush as you walk through a store and a pair of shoes catches your eye? All of a sudden you slow down and magically have an extra five or ten minutes to try them on. This is what can happen when you're working to move your prospects along the conversion chain.

HOW TO GO FROM TALK TO TABLE

Whether your lead has been converted from a text conversation or you started with the phone call itself, the goal is to get to the table. In other words, to schedule an appointment. Remember, the table we're talking about here is the kitchen table in the seller's house. When we get to working with buyers, the table will be in your space, but to keep this simple, we're staying focused on sellers for now.

You will speak to people seeking all kinds of information, but in a lead generation context, a few common scenarios will play out. For example, some people will ask directly about selling their home, and others will inquire about listings already on the market. Just remember to keep the goal of scheduling an appointment top of mind. It's common for agents to get so wrapped up in being helpful and informative that the conversation ends without them even asking for an appointment.

When you're on the phone, the first move is to recap what you talked about digitally. From that point, continue trading information with them until all of their questions seem to be answered. They ask a question, you answer them and then ask your own return question. It's the same pattern you were following initially. And as that conversation is playing out, your job is to listen for an opening to solve a problem.

The way you do that is to offer a sales magnet that provides critical information they are missing. The simplest way to think of this is when a seller wants to sell but isn't sure what their home is worth. In that case, you could offer what we theorize is our industry's first sales magnet, the comparative market analysis, as discussed earlier. Often when people ask about active listings, presenting themselves as buyers, they are in fact sellers because they own a home they must sell before buying the next one.

If you get in the habit of asking every supposed buyer about their current home, that information will come out, and rather than getting distracted by their next house, you can focus on going for the listing appointment.

CLOSING FOR THE APPOINTMENT

If closing for an appointment sounds like hard-edge old school sales to you, don't let it trip you up. Here's a modern way of describing it. When you close for an appointment, you're making an offer to give someone information that will make their decision easier. Instead of money, you are charging them time. In this case, time to meet with them in person and see the property.

In short, you give them something helpful; they give you time. It's a balanced trade. You could sum up a prospecting call like this: trade information, offer something of value for free, and ask for time to deliver it.

Specifically, here's how you make the offer:

- ▶ Introduce your sales magnet (such as a CMA).
- ▶ Explain what it will do for them.
- ▶ Propose two times to meet. (This is called an alternate choice close.)

"Mrs. Seller, since you're thinking about selling, let's go over a comparative market analysis together. That way, you'll have up-to-date information about the value of your home as you're making your plans. I can meet you tomorrow around six in the evening, or would Saturday at two be better?"

Sounds pretty simple, right? Well, it's actually very simple, but you must already know, people don't always take your offers the first time. Sometimes they hesitate or outright decline your offer, so to become effective at converting people from talk to table, you'll need to learn to close three times.

When I first learned about closing, it freaked me out because it felt like I would be pushy. Eventually, I learned what all top producers learn: the pushy feeling is all in your head. In practice, when you commit to closing three times, no more and no less, you learn people respect you for being professionally persistent. In fact, people appreciate that persistence because when you are willing to hang in there and ask for an appointment more than once, it gives them the space to work it out in their head.

After all, we're not talking about small ticket items here. For most people, any and all decisions about their home, including a simple decision to sit down with an agent and talk, are big ones. When a person declines your initial offer to meet, your job is to get them to open up and talk to you. That usually takes a few minutes, especially if you haven't met them before.

How then do you ensure you provide space and close three times? You'll need at least three offers—that is, three sales magnets you've created that would be helpful to a seller. The CMA is one, so you'll need a minimum of two more or there's no way you'll close three times. This is where your creativity takes over because, as we discussed, you are only limited by your imagination.

If I were you, I'd start a journal or online document that was exclusively for your ideas that may one day turn into usable sales magnets. But in case you've missed it, we already covered three. The CMA is one and because it's the easiest, it's the one I always recommend offering first. The real estate market timer was the second, and the maximum market price forecaster was the third.

You'll also need to get good at asking open-ended questions to continue a conversation. When a seller declines your first offer, asking an open-ended question will keep the conversation going. Here are a couple of examples. "What else is on your mind regarding your move?" or "Where else are you researching information on your move?" Almost any question that gets them talking again will suffice.

It takes time and practice to get good at this. It also takes a clear understanding of the sales magnets you have available to you and what they will do for the consumer. The CMA helps a seller understand the current market value of their home. The maximum market price analysis helps assure they are asking the highest possible price they can without pushing too far. The real estate market timer helps them expertly plan the timing of their move.

A useful exercise is to take the time to list all of your sales magnets and then write out the benefit to the client if they take the offer and actually use the information you give them. The clearer you are on what you can offer, the easier it will be for you to put sales magnets to use. And the more you practice asking open-ended questions to keep the seller engaged, the easier it will become to move through a conversation and close three times.

If, after the third attempt, they still decline to meet with you, move on and follow up later. I've never been an advocate of the close-until-you-get-it line of thinking. In fact, that would most likely damage a relationship, but I've never seen any harm done by closing three times.

The Listing Appointment: What You'll Never Learn from Reality TV

PREPARING FOR THE APPOINTMENT

Once a person agrees to meet with you, new energy is injected into the call and it's important to take advantage of it. Early in my career, when I'd schedule an appointment, I'd quickly get off the phone, holler out "got one," and strut around the office talking off my rush of adrenaline, most likely irritating everyone around me.

But then I'd get to these appointments and learn I was facing some roadblocks I wasn't prepared to handle. For example, I'd discover the spouse wasn't there so there was literally no way I'd get a completed agreement. Or that the seller thought their home was worth so much more than the market indicated, a meeting was almost pointless. Other times, I'd be told "something came up" and they only had twenty minutes to chat.

The high of getting an appointment was replaced by the low of realizing I'd wasted a huge amount of time. Eventually

I learned to take all of that adrenaline I felt when the seller agreed to meet and channel it back into the call to make sure my appointment was set up for success.

Ultimately, this amounted to establishing appointment standards. Given all the effort you will no doubt put into each of your appointments, you also deserve to have some basic standards met before you invest your time preparing. At a minimum you deserve the following:

▶ To have all owners present for the meeting
▶ To have two hours of time scheduled
▶ To have a clear understanding of what they feel their home is worth
▶ To have enough information about the property to ballpark the CMA

Setting up high-quality appointments is as simple as being willing to ask a few more questions after you've scheduled a time to meet. Obviously, if you agree you deserve to have these standards met, then you'll be asking about other owners and confirming they will be there. You'll also be asking them to describe their home so you can do your research, and you'll ask them what they feel their house is worth. How you ask is less important than that you ask in the first place.

You don't need to be given a list of questions if you internalize these standards. You can come up with your own questions and phrase them in a way that fits your unique personality. The only standard that trips people up initially is getting an appointment scheduled for two hours. So if your appointment is for 5:00 p.m., ask if they have any other plans between 5:00 and 7:00. They will usually say no, so then tell them you're going to block off that time on your calendar so they have plenty of time to ask you questions. Ask them to block it off on theirs as well and indicate you'll use as much or as little of the time as is needed. This way you get two hours of their time without having to directly ask for it.

As you learn to run high-level listing appointments, you'll see that you often only need sixty to ninety minutes to do it well. But sometimes, you need more time to handle all the objections that come up.

FROM TABLE TO TERMS

Going from an in-person meeting at the table to a signed representation agreement means you've made the third conversion. By comparison, the third conversion is vastly more complex than the first two. So much more complex that you'll spend the rest of your career in fascination at the endless levels of mastery there are to achieve.

Mastery is the ability to perform a skill so well that the body has taken over for the mind. For example, your body knows how to drive. It knows how to speak your native language. It knows how to play tennis (if that's your sport), or it knows how to do whatever hobby you do all the time. At one time, though, all those tasks required a lot of mental effort. Interestingly, everyone who masters a skill eventually runs into an experience that shakes them out of their unconscious mindset and reveals new levels of mastery to achieve.

That's why you never truly master anything as such. You are never really done, and nowhere in sales is this easier to see than it is in the last conversion from table to terms. When you start attending appointments, you quickly learn that each person you work with and each meeting you run will be unique.

So the real objective of your appointment is to get a signed agreement, right? Actually no.

I can promise you now that if, on every appointment you attend, your goal is to get a signature, you're going to burn out fast. The goal of every appointment is to get a yes or to get a no. Chronic underperformers walk away from most of their appointments with a maybe, which is why in the next section, we're going to break down the sales process so that you have a clear path to getting a decision from the seller either way.

SETTING YOUR MIND FOR APPOINTMENTS

To perform at a high level, you must attend appointments with the right mindset. This doesn't happen automatically so you have to set your mind for what you're about to do. For example, on the days when Serena Williams is playing in a major tournament final, she doesn't wake up and try to get as much done as she can before the match. I don't know her routine, but I do know that every champion has one, and it serves to prepare them for the most important part of that day.

As easy as that is to understand in sports, for some reason, in business, people spend almost no time setting their mind before game time. Unfortunately, many in our industry are constantly running seven minutes late for everything. We have the best intentions, I know. We're trying to tend to a million little details, I get that. But if you are the person who's always seven minutes late for your appointments, it sends a signal to your clients that you're more important than they are.

Ouch.

You are the boss and you must control your schedule. You must know how to stop a task or an appointment and leave enough time to get to the next task. And I don't mean just enough time to drive through traffic. I mean, enough time to drive and mentally prep yourself. If Serena has to do it, so do you. It's in the client's best interest and it's in yours. Think of it this way. Serena has probably forgotten more about the game of tennis than most people will ever learn, but even at her level, if she shows up mentally unprepared, her knowledge isn't going to take her that far.

Likewise, I could teach you everything I know about sales, but if you show up to appointments rushed and unprepared mentally, my coaching won't help you much.

THE SALES APPOINTMENT,
THE SELLER'S PSYCHOLOGICAL JOURNEY

The sales appointment itself is my favorite part of being an agent, but it wasn't always that way. Like everyone else, when I first started attending appointments, I was terrified. Not only was I learning a new skill, but I was barely twenty years old and still had plenty of acne that did nothing but broadcast my youth and make me feel insecure. Because no one gave me a process to follow, I was flying by the seat of my pants. On the rare occasion I was able to schedule an appointment, my fear and insecurities were felt energetically by the prospective client. So it won't surprise you to learn I wasn't hired on any of my early listing appointments.

But then I was taught that I could follow a four-step process and, more importantly, that process would do the heavy lifting for me. At that point I wasn't interested in why it worked, only that it did. Once I started using the process, sales began to turn around quickly. I'd still be met at the front door of the property with great hesitation when the seller saw I was so young. But a few minutes into the appointment, when they could sense that I knew what I was doing and actually had control of the situation, the energy shifted, and I could literally see them relax in front of my eyes. On those appointments, I was able to transform from an acne-ridden kid they'd accidentally scheduled an appointment with to a young tiger (their words) who would help them get started.

You might not be eighteen, but you no doubt have your version of limiting beliefs to overcome. Clearly, it didn't matter that I was eighteen with crippled confidence and little to no experience. Those aspects were never the real problem. The state of Texas said it was legal for me to do business, and once I learned the process, I began to take listings regularly. All it took was a little coaching, a little skill, and a mindset adjustment.

Take a minute and think about your inner dialogue. Whether you're reading this on day one of your career or day 1,001, what stories do you tell yourself that hold you back from your full potential? Is there something about your appearance that you don't like? Is it your experience level that makes you feel inadequate? Have you too often compared yourself to other agents in your market who you think are more deserving? Do you tell yourself you're too young? Or too old? What about your gender or economic status? Do you feel life would be easier if you were the opposite sex or if you came from a family with more money and connections?

The sales appointment is a journey for your prospects and you are the guide. When you take complete ownership of your role as the guide, you don't have the time to indulge your limiting beliefs and the focus shifts onto the prospect where it belongs. Once they sense that has happened—if they ever cared at all about those things you thought they did—they have stopped.

FOUR-PART SALES PROCESS

When it comes to the sales appointment, whether it's a routine they fall into or deliberately designed, everyone has a process. The average agent never steps back to see if their routine is an effective one for them. To prove this, just ask any random person in your office what their conversion rate is on listing appointments. Sadly, most won't know and may never have been coached to pay attention.

On the other end of the scale, you'll find people who boast that they get every listing appointment they attend. Truth be told, that's their ego talking so don't believe it when you hear it. And if you can find a person who really does take 100 percent of the listing appointments they attend, they are likely taking overpriced listings they shouldn't or only going on appointments where the listing falls into their lap.

The process you're about to learn is not intended to set you up for a 100 percent conversion rate. That would mean you've given all your power away and are willing to work with anyone, even people you don't particularly like. That would also be the opposite reason why most people got into the business. If you have to work on whatever projects come your way, you might as well be an employee.

The process will create the space necessary for you to make conscious decisions about whether you believe you can effectively help the prospect or if you even want to take them on as clients. Depending on where you are in your business when you read this, that statement could sound liberating or crazy. If you've been working your butt off for years, it can be refreshing to hear that you don't have to operate from a scarcity-based mindset. Trying to work with every single person that comes your way whether you enjoy it or not is no fun and not sustainable.

If that's you, mastering the four-part sales process will immediately begin improving your conversion rate. When you have to go on fewer appointments to bring in the business you have decided you need, you are liberated and feel like you can turn down business you don't want. The most common example of this is when an agent stops trying to work listings all over their market and instead narrows their focus to the area of town they have always wanted to specialize in and truly enjoy.

If you are newer or in a slump, then every lead and transaction is going to feel super critical. Everyone has been there at some point, including me. The good news is that when you make a commitment to mastering the four-part sales process, your confidence skyrockets and your overall levels of optimism and hope increase. It may take you longer than more productive agents to pivot, but that's only temporary as you build momentum. At any point in time, you have to remember that momentum comes first, skill comes second.

We could work together until you understand sales like your native language, but if you never go on appointments, it won't matter. It'd be like sitting in a room by yourself speaking this beautiful language that no one can hear.

The four-part sales process also has a ton of benefits for the prospect. Just as it creates space for you to make your decisions, it makes space for the client to make theirs. A masterful sales appointment is balanced between the needs of the salesperson and the prospect. When a person has decided to sell their home, they've entered into territory that is highly unfamiliar. They've likely mentioned the move to friends and family, and you can be sure everyone around them has an opinion on what they should do. Now they've invited a stranger (you) over to their home to discuss a topic that impacts the deepest levels of their personal and financial lives.

I want you to understand how big this is for a prospective seller, even if on the surface they seem cool as a cucumber. Specifically, each seller will go through a psychological journey with four distinct stages:

- ▶ No way, Jose.
- ▶ I never thought of it that way.
- ▶ I think you can help me.
- ▶ I'm glad you came over.

When you first get to the property, the seller is in a mental state of "No way, Jose." Like, no way am I going to sign anything tonight and sometimes they even blurt that out. The sales process creates the space for you to guide them on this journey so that at the end they are in a mental state of "I'm glad you came over." That's the mental state that gets signatures on listing agreements.

Think about appointments you've been on in the past. When you walked away with the listing, it meant the seller traveled that journey successfully. When you walked away without a listing because they wanted to think it over, it meant at some point they got lost and confused. I think the greatest part about what you're learning now is that from this point forward, you can expertly guide your prospects so they no longer get lost.

In other words, you no longer have to worry about getting a listing. Your only concern will be staying on track. That kind of focus will set you up to get the signature or it will help you determine that you should not take the listing. Or maybe that you just don't want it.

Can you imagine running your business that way? What would happen if you never again stressed out about an appointment and instead let the process do all the work for you? Even if it's hard for you to picture at this moment, I can promise you that, eventually, the confidence and positive, client-first energy you project will, in and of itself, increase your conversion rate, even if you don't always follow the process to a T or get mixed up while you're learning.

The sales process has four parts that correspond perfectly with the psychological journey of the seller and I'll break down each one. They are

▶ Take Control
▶ Find the Problem
▶ Solve the Problem
▶ Close

Step One: Take Control

Your main objectives in this step are to get the seller to relax into the environment you are creating and lay out the agenda for the meeting. I can't emphasize this enough: if you don't take control of your appointments up front, you will never get control of them.

Taking control starts in your own mind by remembering that it's impossible to walk into a listing appointment knowing in advance that you want to take the listing. Most agents walk into each appointment truly hoping they get it and carry an almost desperate energy around with them. Top producers, however, know better and keep their distance emotionally. They understand that there are many avenues to investigate before it's possible to know if they want the listing.

Would you want a listing even if it's grossly overpriced? Difficult to show? What if the owners are argumentative or closed off and don't seem to want to open up to you? What if you just determine you don't like them or their property? You don't need every listing and you can't work them all anyway, so if the seller starts the appointment with a "No way, Jose" attitude, it's balanced by your wait-and-see mindset.

Once you arrive at the property, your goal is to get to the kitchen table. Where you meet is important because family and close friends gather in the kitchen; whereas, others traditionally gather in the living room. To get to the kitchen, just start walking in that direction. A simple, "Let's get started in the kitchen. It's this way, isn't it?" will do. The seller doesn't know you have a process and they don't really know how this is supposed to go so they'll instinctively follow you.

If anything, they may think you want to start by looking at the house and may even ask if you want to do that. After all, your competition started by looking at the property, which is even more reason you should not. One of the benefits of taking control in this way is that you set yourself apart from every other agent they've met.

Once you're at the kitchen table, don't be afraid to start clearing it off if needed. That may sound aggressive but, again, as long as you move confidently, they'll follow right along. A clean meeting space is part of the environment you are designing for them. What comes next might be the hardest part of taking control and that is to sit down and talk to them. You know, chitchat, small talk. Untrained salespeople get right down to business, and when they do, they make a huge mistake.

You have no clue what went on in their day and what was happening right before you arrived. Moving is stressful so it's possible there was tension between partners, or one of them had to rush home in traffic. Maybe they had a rough day at work or are worried about the trouble their kid got into at school earlier. Now, here you are in their house and they are out of their family's routine. They need time to settle into this environment or they won't be listening to anything you say.

Think about the last time you were running late for a meeting. No doubt you felt irritated by the event that delayed you. Then there was an adrenaline surge as you rushed to get where you're supposed to be and then the guilty feelings the first few moments you arrive as everyone already there has turned and looked at you in judgment—or at least that's what you felt, right? How long did it take you to settle down and be truly present in the room? It certainly wasn't instantly.

Every appointment you attend will need space created for the prospect to become fully present with you, and the only way to do that is to look them in the eye and simply talk. Ask them about their day. If you saw amazing flower beds when you arrived, ask about that. If you saw a moose over the fireplace on the way to the kitchen, ask about that. Salespeople are supposed to be good at striking up a conversation, so now is the time to be a conversationalist.

One way people release anxious or nervous energy is to talk. If you arrive calm and focused, not trying to get a listing and are willing to slow down enough to establish rapport, you'll be setting yourself up for success. It may take you some time and practice to get good at it, but once you do, you'll find this first step natural and enjoyable. In fact, one day you'll notice that you are calm enough to observe yourself grounding their nervous energy.

Your next goal is to determine when they are ready to move

forward. They aren't going to verbally tell you they're relaxed and ready, but they will show you by physically relaxing. You might notice they have uncrossed their arms or relaxed their shoulders and leaned back in the chair away from the table. It's possible you'll notice them laugh and smile or they might ask about your day or offer you something to drink. When you allow someone the space to relax and open up to you, they stop worrying so much about you trying to convince them to sign an agreement and instead lower their wall to make a real connection.

In any case, the moment you see they are ready, it's time to get down to business. Just as they signaled to you by shifting their body language that they are present, you signal to them that it's time to work by shifting yours. You don't have to be overly dramatic but sit up in your chair a little more and grab whatever you use to take notes and display your presentation visuals.

Next you are going to directly address their fear that you are there just to get them to sign a listing agreement. It sounds like, "I'm not here to convince you to list your home just so I can walk away with a new listing. I don't even know yet if I can help you. I'm here to work with you to discover what would be the best for your family long term."

That's a kind of takeaway close that sets you apart even further because you're already demonstrating you understand what's likely on their mind. What are you here to do again? Guide them through a process and get them ready to go through it. The last two steps you'll do to take control of the appointment is to use a concept called fear of loss, then literally lay out the agenda for the appointment.

Fear of loss is a powerful motivator when you use it ethically in your practice. To understand fear of loss, consider whether you'd work harder to save $2,000 or to prevent some-one from stealing $2,000 from you, as introduced earlier. If you're like most other humans, you'd initially work to prevent theft, wouldn't you? Fear of loss is baked into the human con-dition so you might as well use it for the good of everyone on your appointment.

Using fear of loss is ethical when it's the method used to frame a discussion in a way that gives the seller a healthy and objective perspective. Sellers think their house is the most spe-cial one ever and never consider that it won't sell. But even in the strongest economies, we all know there is still an expired category in the MLS. That expired list is going to be one of your most important tools.

When you are selling, it's always more effective to show somebody something than it is to tell them something. In other words, you could talk about the expired list, but it would be much better if you show it to them. When I first learned this, we used dot matrix printers in the office. Those are all in museums now, but have you ever seen the printers that used paper with holes on each side and perforations such that you had to tear each page apart? I was able to print the expired list so that I had a huge stack of paper.

These days, I'd likely print the expired list to a PDF docu-ment that was long enough I could scroll almost endlessly on my iPad. The expired list is only a visual used to make your point so it doesn't matter when the properties expired, only that they did and that you have a huge list of them.

Specifically, the point you want to make is that the deci-sions made during the meeting will either get them on the sold list or the expired list. They think all they are doing is inter-viewing agents and aren't even considering the fact their house might not sell if they make the wrong decisions. Your job is to reframe the appointment from the act of simply interviewing agents to a collaborative process where important decisions are made.

Picture taking your expired list and flicking your finger on the screen to scroll through a seemingly endless list as you describe all the experiences sellers go through when their home is on the market, all of it in vain. Your goal is to help them see that some sellers go through six months of disruption only to end up canceling their plans. If your seller goes through the rest of the appointment making decisions based on what will keep them off the expired list, you'll have served them at a very high level.

It's important to acknowledge what has happened up to this point. You've created space so they could relax into the environment and become truly present. You've set yourself apart from your competition in a big way just by doing that. Then you directly addressed the fear they didn't even realize you were aware of when you said you weren't there just to get a listing. When you do this, you are meeting them in the conversation already going on in their head and it's incredibly powerful. Marketing professionals spend entire careers working on doing that with the ads they create.

And to truly anchor that point, you even implied that you might not offer your services. That depends on whether you determine you can truly help them or not. Once again, you're further distancing yourself from your competition who was no doubt focused primarily on trying to get the listing. Next, you snapped them to attention by completely reframing the conversation. If you're there to help them determine the best path forward, you suggested that the decisions made are less about getting the house sold and more about avoiding decisions that will cause them to end up on the expired list. That is a subtle but powerful message. You've essentially suggested that under the right conditions, you already know you can sell the house. On a pure business level, I know you understand that. If they price the house correctly, it will sell. There's no magic to this.

Next we need to put an agenda in place that will provide a framework for the rest of the listing appointment. Think of this agenda as specifically how you will take your clients through the four stages of the sales process. It will also keep you on the track everyone can refer back to if the appointment spins off in a crazy direction.

While all sales appointments go through the four general stages, the agenda you use to accomplish that can change from situation to situation. For example, later on I'll discuss a separate agenda for your buyer consultations. It'll look different but, at the end of the day, still guides your clients through the four general stages of a sales appointment.

This may be the easiest visual you'll ever create in your business. You either open up a Word document or a fresh slide on your presentation software and type out these six steps:

- ▶ Step One: Deep dive into your family's goal
- ▶ Step Two: Deep dive into your property
- ▶ Step Three: How we'll find your buyer
- ▶ Step Four: Finding your highest price and what you get at closing
- ▶ Step Five: How we get started
- ▶ Step Six: Making a mutual decision

When I first saw this process many years ago, I could barely sit still. Finally after almost two years I felt like I was let in on a big secret to listings. The trick here is to use your visual to explain the six steps as an overview of the appointment. You aren't going to do all of them at this moment; you're only giving them the road map.

This plan benefits both you and your prospective seller in several ways. First, it removes the anxiety of the unknown. If you don't tell them what's going to happen, they'll have to try and anticipate as you go and people really hate doing that. It's why at my father's funeral, the director came to me and explained how the day would unfold step-by-step. Importantly, he also told me that I didn't have to remember any of it. When we were done with one step, he'd be right there to guide me on what to do next.

That may seem like an extreme example, but I can't tell you how grateful I was for his step-by-step system while I was under that stress. In the same, albeit maybe less intense way, your step-by-step system will put the minds of your prospective sellers at ease. Second, it makes it much easier for you to remain in control during the appointment. Remember, you're not there just to get the listing. Yes, you want as many of those as you can get but not just any listing. You're there to control the appointment so everyone can make the best decisions possible. Because you're the professional, it's your responsibility to maintain control.

Step Two: Find the Problem

Now that you have control of the appointment, it's time to get to work discovering the problem you're there to solve. Here's a hint: the problem is not that they have a house they need sold. We'll come back to that thought.

But, first, to become truly masterful at sales, it's important to understand that if your prospects don't see your services as a direct solution to their problem, as they uniquely define it in their mind, they won't hire you. Nearly every person you consider your competition will spend little if any time getting to the root of what the seller wants and why they want it. They will assume that the seller wants to sell for the highest price possible and, because of that assumption, will spend the majority of their time talking about why their company is the best and then getting lost in the weeds of CMA details.

Unfortunately, this misdirection robs the seller of the space they need to continue on their psychological journey. At this point, the seller doesn't think they have a problem other than the need to find an agent they like and trust and, of course, a buyer. Your goal in step two of this process is to help them look deeper into their situation and frame it in a way that gives them greater clarity and focus.

As the professional, you should be thinking much bigger than the client. The solution is on a higher level than the problem, so any agent who simply talks about their marketing, their company, and the CMA is stuck on the same level of thinking as the seller. Why would anyone pay for that? Have you considered this might be one of the reasons agents get asked to lower their commission? Thinking on the same level as the client makes you a commodity.

When I visit my CPA, I'm expecting insight I can't get on my own by reading a financial blog. The only way my CPA can give me that is by taking time to get to know me. He has to go deeper than talking about how he can help me save money on taxes. He has to discover what kind of lifestyle I want my business to fund and why. With that deeper insight, he can lead me to more powerful financial strategies.

Therefore, whether accounting or real estate, the more time any professional spends to get to know their client's deepest desires, the more the client feels heard and even understood. This builds strong loyalty and minimizes objections, including price objections. By that I mean, your price: your commission.

You know you're watching a real pro when you see them spend the majority of their time on an appointment finding, clarifying, and anchoring the problem before they say a word about their services. This is another one of those times when you want to channel your inner five-year-old and get as curious as you can about the seller. If you've been through other sales training, you might have learned this part of the appointment as qualifying the seller, and there's nothing wrong with that classic sales training language, but when I was initially trained, I was given a list of questions and told to ask them in order. If I could manage, I would allow their answers to springboard to others.

For example, if I asked why they were moving and the answer was a job change, I could springboard to questions that would inform me about their profession. This basic pattern served me well for several years. As my own skills improved, I learned that there was a better way to make prospects feel truly understood than simply asking them questions and writing down their answers until I felt I had enough information.

It's called a problem package, which allows you to address the unique concerns of each individual seller. For example, just because a couple is married, doesn't mean they will have the exact same reasons for wanting to move. One may be driven by a need to be closer to work and the other may be primarily concerned with schools that service the area in which they live. There are a set of very common reasons why people move including job changes, births, deaths, marriages, divorces, and more. Life change drives the real estate industry. But each person will think about their situation as unique, even within the same family.

Building the Problem Package

Packaging things up creates order, doesn't it? Think of how satisfying it is to carry a package out of a store. At one point you were navigating through items that were spread out all over the place until you made your choices and worked with a salesperson who placed your final choices in the bag or box, probably with some decorative tissue paper and a stylish sticker to hold it all together. Sometimes there's even a satin ribbon.

Then, when you get home, you get to experience the joy of unwrapping the package. Building a problem package on a listing appointment is the equivalent of wrapping up the package in a store. Later on, you'll unwrap it with them. First let's work on our wrapping skills. You'll build the problem package in four steps: question, clarify, implication, and anchor.

Question: This is the part everyone does naturally but few do really well. As you were setting the appointment and gathering information about the seller and their motivations for moving, you no doubt learned a lot about them. It would be a mistake to assume they remembered anything about that conversation. When you begin asking questions, it's best for the client to just start from the beginning.

An appropriate opening question is this: "Why are you moving?" Although if there is more than one seller, turn to the one you didn't speak to when you set the appointment and ask them to tell you in their own words. You'd be surprised how often the answer differs from each person. [In the website bonuses, I've listed situation questions I used on my appointments to help stimulate your creative juices. You can find all website bonuses at jasenedwards.com/TPLBonus.] To illustrate the rest of the problem package process, we'll stick with the most basic question: "Why are you moving?"

Clarify: Let's pretend the husband's answer to why they are moving is to be closer to his work so he spends less time in traffic and has more time for his family. And let's pretend the wife mentions that her primary reason for moving is getting into a specific school district across town. To serve them at the highest level, you need to know why that's important to them. Simply ask them to explain why.

There are times when it's incredibly easy to assume the reason, and your assumption may in fact be right, but this process is about creating the space for them to vocalize their desires in the context of your appointment. So even if you think you know what they are going to say, give them the space to say it anyway.

Now let's pretend the husband tells you he wants to spend more time with his daughter drawing in the evening, but the wife's concern about the schools is driven by the fact that she wants her child to go to the school that has the best art department in town. When you combine their individual concerns, you get parents who are interested in developing a talent their daughter has exhibited to prepare her for acceptance into a prestigious fine arts college.

So you see, their motivation for moving isn't really about the house at all. People only move because they are drawn to a lifestyle they've envisioned living out once they are in the new property and the boxes are unpacked. The more you get them to talk about that vision during your appointment and the more they sense you are focused on it, the less likely they are to give you objections and the more likely you are to walk out with a listing. In a way, building a problem package could be called objection prevention.

Implication: Remember when I talked about fear of loss before? If you want someone to act, talk about what they'll gain if they do. If you want them to act now, talk about what they'll lose if they don't. So you need to know what would happen if they don't get what they want.

What happens, from their point of view, if the house doesn't sell? Far from being negative, asking implication questions is all about going deep into an understanding of why they want what they want. Questions like "What would happen if the house doesn't sell?" and "Would you give up on this vision you have for your daughter?" demonstrate your sincere attempt to get to the very core of their desires. And their answers will deliver incredible insight into how serious they are about moving.

That's important because, remember, you are there to make a decision as well. The last step on the appointment is where everyone makes a mutual decision, not where you beg for the listing. If the motivation to sell isn't strong enough, you may very well decline to take the listing. Said another way, when you decline to take a listing, it's often because you didn't discover any serious problems. The first time you do that, I want to hear from you. Find me online and send me a message (hello@jasenedwards.com), and wherever I am, we'll find a way to celebrate how you've held your own power. That will be a moment of significant growth in your career.

Anchor: "If we team up, you're saying you want me to focus on—." Now that you've really got their attention and discovered the profoundness of their vision, it's time to anchor it. To anchor their answer is the equivalent of placing an item in the box for wrapping. The way you do it is to repeat what they said back to them and ask for confirmation that you understand what they told you.

"So if we were to team up tonight, I'm hearing you say you want my focus to be getting the home sold so you recapture time lost in traffic and have the ability to enroll your daughter in the best school for her talents. Is that correct?"

It's common at this point for you to see their faces light up because you've just demonstrated you truly understand them. I've heard it said that people have two fundamental desires: they want to be heard and they want to be right. When you take the time to build a problem package with them, you give them a chance to be heard in a way that probably no other agent ever has.

But notice the subtlety in the dialogue. I suggested you say, "if we team up tonight," which basically means you haven't yet decided if you want to take this listing. Statements like this keep the appointment balanced and help you retain your own power so you are less likely to trip into scarcity thinking and take a listing you shouldn't or don't really want.

Now you have a choice to make as the leader of this appointment. Was that item you just placed in the box so precious and important that you need to close it up with tissue paper and ribbon or do you sense they have other items? Most of the time, they are going to have other items for their box, so go back to your list of situation questions and consider what else you want to hear them expand on.

The fun part about this is that you can take it in any direction you want since you're in control. With an issue like schools, it would be smart to ask them about timing. So you may ask: "By when do you need to be settled in your new home?"

Your next step then is to clarify. I know you know why timing is important for schools, but still you don't want to rob them of the chance to be heard. You know they are going to tell you there is an enrollment deadline, but it would be a mistake if you don't let them say it. Of course then you ask them what would happen if they missed the deadline (the implication) and then place that item in the package. In other words, anchor it by repeating back what you heard.

"Okay so I should also be mindful of the timing so your family can be settled before the next school year starts, correct?"

Wrapping the Package

The general rule is that the more items you put into the problem package, the more the seller is going to feel like you truly understand them. You can cycle through as many situational questions as you want or need to until you feel you've sufficiently uncovered all of the items that are important to the seller. Each problem you uncover is simply a part of the vision they have of their life after they are resettled, from the point of view of it being missing.

Said another way, the problem package you've built helps them crystalize why they want what they say they want. You know that every deal doesn't go exactly as the seller expects it to, but they don't initially see it that way, and this reframe will highlight the importance of the decisions being made on the listing appointment. Wrapping up the package doesn't take long at all, it's just a metaphor for recapping what you've learned and transitioning to the next item on your agenda—looking at the property. "So to recap, here's what I've learned about your vision—."

Over time, you'll develop the skill necessary to sense when you have uncovered enough about them and their situation. On some appointments this will be simple, and on others it will be like peeling back the layers of an onion. Give yourself some grace as your skills develop. This is really high-level selling and worth all the time it takes to get really good at it.

Step Three: Solve the Problem

Next on your listing appointment agenda is to look through the property. After you've done that and taken your notes, it's time to go back to the kitchen table where you will unwrap your problem package and demonstrate how you will solve each problem for them.

If people aren't sold on the idea that you're the best person to help them realize their vision, you won't be hired. It's as simple as that. Now that you have a clear understanding of what they really want and what they'll have to do to get it, and now that the seller is looking at their situation from the correct frame of mind, you are perfectly positioned to sell your services as the solution.

Most agents think of this part of the appointment as the marketing presentation. But rather than narrowly focusing on marketing for the house, the marketing tactics you show them in this step are presented so the seller sees them as the tools you use to get them to their new lifestyle. You're going to learn how to continually reinforce in their minds that you are zeroed in on the life they wish to be living in their new home. When you do this, you become unique and unlike any other agent they've met before and you become inexpensive by comparison.

Commission objections are minimized when you execute this step well. Why does a new Porsche 911 start at $97,400? Not because the average person thinks it's worth that but because it solves very specific problems for those who buy one, even if that problem is only temporary relief during a midlife crisis. This step of the process makes you the Porsche 911.

To me, this is the easiest step of the entire appointment process in which to gain an advantage over your competition because it's the one most commonly squandered. Most agents are led to believe that the best way to handle this part of the listing presentation is to talk about how great their company is, show the seller a few marketing tactics, go over the CMA, and then maybe ask for a signature. And most who do that leave the appointment a prisoner of hope as the seller thinks about it.

Sometimes they get a call back but usually they don't. It's not even the fault of the agent who is just doing what they've been taught or what they've been able to observe and piece together from various examples. Most sellers will be given presentations full of boasting about how great the agent and company is, complete with awards given to both the broker and the agent, alongside marketing tactics that the seller finds about as interesting as yesterday's weather report.

There's nothing wrong with talking about your accomplishments. A seller wants you to be reasonably successful after all, but they don't really care if you're the company top producer or not. That's because sellers are tuned into a completely different frequency. If it were a radio station, the station would be called WIIFM (What's In It for Me?). If you want to communicate with the seller on a meaningful level, especially at this stage of the appointment, you must tune into their frequency because they won't be tuning into yours.

This step is also important because when you're not broadcasting your message on their frequency, you force them to price shop. These days there is a lot of discussion on the downward pressure on agent commissions. The prevailing opinion is that technology will disrupt the traditional compensation model. And maybe it will but that doesn't necessarily mean you will have to make less.

This may not be the perfect comparison, but Tesla, with its disrupting automobile technology, didn't suddenly make Porsche go broke. It didn't even force Porsche to reduce the price of the 911. Porsche changed with the times and solved a new problem by releasing the Taycan, an electric car for people who still want a Porsche. And it has a starting price $6,400 higher than the 911, which still sells very well.

The primary problem individual agents have with their fee has far less to do with technology disruptions and more with how, as an industry, we force sellers to price shop us. Because most of us are taught to show sellers why we (and our companies) are the best, then show them some marketing tactics, we come off looking essentially the same as everyone else, but with different colors on our signs.

Think about this for a minute. What can you do to find a buyer for a home that another agent can't? Everyone has access to the same tools. At the end of the day, you may actually do more than other agents, but it's the price that sells the home, not your marketing. Your marketing simply finds you your next set of leads. Need proof? Take the most overpriced home in your market and spend your life's savings on ads placed on *Good Morning America*. Then the house will sell, right? Clearly not.

Houses sell because they are priced correctly, and the seller will always think you are marketing their home in order to sell it. In the aggregate you are because collectively, as agents advertise listings, they drum up buyer leads and some of those leads buy houses. As a business owner you have to be clear that your primary reason for advertising a listing is to generate leads.

I'll talk about this more in the next section, but for now it's important to get comfortable with the disparity between your business reason for running advertising and the seller's assumptions about why you do it. Both points of view can exist without conflict, and it's okay for a seller to lack some understanding of your business operations. Ultimately, they just want to reach their goal, and it's why you need a powerful way to communicate you are the best person to help them.

Solution Selling

In order to tune into their frequency, you'll make your marketing presentation through a framework called solution selling: point, transition, solution, and agreement.

Following the solution selling framework prevents you from "talking at" the seller and instead keeps you in a conversation with them. Talking at people is one-way communication and literally forces people to tune out. The framework is also your secret weapon to selling your services as the solution to their problem. It's worth emphasizing this because happy customers say nice things, but successful customers will send you referrals. Helping your clients move from one place to another will make them happy and they might leave you a five-star review online. The problem with stopping there in your thinking is that it's all about the property.

Helping your clients move from one place to another while constantly speaking to the vision in their head and how you're guiding them to that vision step-by-step will make them feel successful. That subtle but incredibly powerful shift puts people first. A few people in every company can do this intuitively. If that's you, great. This section will just confirm your natural talent. If that's not you, and it wasn't me either, the great news is that you can learn how.

Making Your Point: The first step is to make a point or state a fact of some kind. This is what everyone does automatically. We make statements about the approaches we'll do to market a property. We say "we use professional stagers" or "we use lifestyle videos." What usually goes along with this is a visual of some kind that we show the seller and a short description of the tactic. Average salespeople will simply move on to the next point until they get to the end of their marketing presentation. But top producers go deeper.

Transition: This is fast and simple. It's just a set of words that moves your dialogue forward and makes you sound smooth. The textbook phrase is, "What that means to you is—." But there are tons of variations including but not limited to, "How that will benefit you is—," "What that will do for you is—," "That will get you closer to your vision because—," "This will really help you because—," "You'll love this one because—."

The more transition phrases you have on the tip of your tongue, the more natural you'll sound. When I first learned this technique, I could hear myself on appointments using "What this means to you is—" way too much. But that phrase was all I could get out of my mouth initially. It was a little awkward for sure, but never prevented me from getting a signature, and because I pushed through the awkwardness, it wasn't long before I developed verbal dexterity with several transitional phrases. The same will happen to you, so don't get too hung up on how you sound at first.

Solution: This is where you nail down the idea that you are the solution to their problem. Remember, anything you bring up in the marketing portion of your presentation must be sent to them on the correct frequency: WIIFM. In other words, to answer what's in it for them, you need to explain how said marketing tactic will help them successfully achieve the vision in their head about the life they'll be living in the new home.

I'll bet I'm the first person who's asked you to explain your marketing in terms the seller can understand, and doing so can be frustrating at first. That's why most of your competition will never do it. Your opportunity is to invest the time wrestling over the words until they flow naturally, and I promise they eventually will.

Agreement: The agreement step is also very simple. Your goal is to get them to grunt. Well, not literally, but if all you can do is get them to grunt, you'll be on track. You do this by using tie down questions and the textbook question everyone starts with is "Does that make sense to you?" Of course, just like in the transition step, you'll need several phrases to sound natural. Alternatives are "Can you see how that would help us?" "Would you be okay with us filming a video in your home?" "Do you see why I get excited about this one?" "Are you picking up what I'm putting down?"

The more appointments you attend, the faster this will become second nature to you. One day you'll effortlessly speak like this:

[POINT] One of my favorite marketing tactics we'll use to promote your home is the lifestyle video. Lifestyle videos are modern versions of virtual tours. Rather than just a video of the rooms in your home, these videos tell a story of what it's like to live here.

[TRANSITION] You're really going to love this because—.

[SOLUTION] These videos play on the emotions of buyers and cause more inquiries. The more inquiries we get, the more likely it is you'll be in your new home before school starts, and you'll be laughing at all the people who are still stuck in traffic.

[AGREEMENT] Would you be okay with us filming in your home?

Lessons from a Bobblehead Jesus: A tie down question is classic sales training, and it's designed to get a minor agreement. It doesn't require a huge enthusiastic response, but when you ask a tie down question, the seller can't just stare at you with a blank expression. They have to at least make some noise, like a grunt, signaling they heard you. Get it?

Tie down questions keep people involved. Have you ever been on an appointment and realized you've been talking for so long their eyes have glazed over? That's a massive danger zone for a salesperson.

One day many years ago, I was driving to a venue to teach a session on this topic in Oklahoma. As I pulled into the parking lot, I noticed most of the cars had bobbleheads on their dashboard. Not just random bobbleheads either. These were all little figures of Jesus's head. Clearly, I'd be speaking in the same venue as a religious convention that day.

As I was explaining solution selling, I asked if anyone else saw all those bobbleheads. Most did so we talked about how the figure would bobble around as long as the car was active. If the car stopped, eventually the figure would stop as well. So we played a game where the agents paired up and practiced asking tie down questions to get agreement.

One person was the agent, and after asking the tie down question, their instruction was to gently tap the nose of their partner. The partner's instruction was to bobble their head and grunt signifying they were still listening to the agent. To this day I still get messages from past clients who laugh because they envision their sellers with springs for necks at that part of their appointment.

Step Four: Close

Transitioning into the closing process starts with what's called a trial close. On a listing appointment, my favorite trial close is this one: "Based on what you've seen so far, if we can agree on price, would anything stop you from hiring me tonight?"

If you've never used a trial close like that before, you'll be shocked by how many times people will respond positively to it. When you take control of an appointment and keep your focus on the best interest of the seller instead of worrying about getting a listing, they feel that energy and become drawn to you. And when you let the sales process provide the space for their psychological journey, they feel safe moving forward.

I don't want to lead you to believe that everyone falls right into line at this point. Many will, but some sellers will signal potential objections when you use that particular trial close. They may tell you they have other agents scheduled to come over or that they will need to think about it. I'm going to cover how to deal with that objection in detail in a bit. For now, asking the question (or your version of it) is important because their response tells you how the rest of the appointment will go. If they are super agreeable, it should be as simple as moving through the next step in the sales process, getting a signature, and moving on.

If you sense there will be objections, you have time to think about how you'll handle them if you decide you want this listing. In other words, if you hear objections at this point, don't address them directly. Just acknowledge that you've heard them and signal you'll come back to their concern. Remember, stay on track and let the process do the work for you. Until you agree on price, you can't be in a position to offer your services, so it's pointless to handle an objection.

The pricing presentation is the official start of the closing process. If you think of the listing appointment agenda, discussing price and net is step four. Steps four through six on the agenda make up the closing portion of your sales process where the key is to move assumptively and confidently through them. Your pricing discussion flows right into an overview of the forms you use and that flows into your mutual decision, at which point you'll ask for their signature, if you've determined you want to work for them.

When you're operating on a really high level, this is where you'll shift the energy of your appointment. The easiest way to understand this is to think of the path of an airplane. In the beginning when you are taking control, you are building momentum into the appointment and that takes a lot of mental energy, just like a plane must burn a ton of fuel to get off the ground.

By the time you've looked around the home and are back at the kitchen table using the solution selling framework for your marketing presentation, you should be on autopilot. Like a plane that has reached cruising altitude, not as much fuel is needed. When a plane is ready to land, the pilot doesn't suddenly dive toward the ground and slam onto the runway. Instead there is a gradual descent over many miles and sometimes when the pilot hits the runway just right, it's so smooth the passengers applaud.

That's what can happen if you hit the energy of the close just right—your prospective sellers will clap. Well, not literally but that's the energetic equivalent of their signing your listing agreement and becoming official clients.

SECRETS TO PRICING PRESENTATIONS– THE REAL TRUTH ABOUT CMAS

Like a good agent, you did your homework and are prepared with a beautiful looking CMA, right? Maybe you've got a slick new app that creates animated charts showing what's going on in the market or maybe you've printed a really classy looking CMA on super-high-quality paper and had it professionally bound. What if I told you all of that was unnecessary and sometimes harmful to both you and the seller?

When it comes to pricing, you have to know that sellers are looking at data before you get in front of them at their kitchen table, and they have formed an opinion about price. If you disagree with them even a little, they are very likely to see any data you show them as cherry picked in an attempt to get them to price the home for a quick sale so you collect a commission.

Remember when you went through all that effort at the beginning of the appointment to get them to relax and lower their walls? Well, if you get this part wrong, those walls are going right back up. What I'm saying is that most of the guidance you've ever been given on discussing price has basically been people telling you to dive bomb the plane onto the run-way. Most agents I've ever coached have learned from people who didn't understand this themselves or, worse, from technology companies who build these products with literally zero understanding of what it's like to be on a listing appointment. You can use apps for your CMA if you want, but by the time you're finished with this section, you'll see that you don't really need any of them. I'm even going to teach you how to have a pricing conversation and never pull out the CMA if you don't have to. Imagine how much time that could save you over a year.

Next, I want you to understand that pricing a home is not scientific. I understand that market analysis apps and appraisals make the process seem scientific, especially when we have standardized methods used by the appraisal industry like the comparison approach, cost approach, or income capitalization approach. We all instinctively know that regardless of what any of these approaches tell us a home should be worth, we never really know until the moment a buyer and seller agree on a sale. That means all of those varying methods lead to nothing more than the opinion of value of the person who prepared the report.

You could take one property and line up two agents and two appraisers, and, although everyone works off the same available data, you would not get four identical opinions of price. This should be a freeing thought for you. I've watched agents get really stressed over the preparation of a market analysis. Some struggle with the technology itself, and others worry about the choice of comps and how to choose them.

So if a market analysis isn't scientific, how can you prepare one without too much added stress? Most people will be working with the comparison approach so we'll stick with that method. The most effective way to prepare a CMA is to start with a narrow search and expand the parameters until you feel you have the data you need. To do that, pull up the neighborhood of the subject property and just stare at the data on the screen. Look at active, pending, and solds.

How far you look back depends on the market. In a strong buyer's market you look back further than a strong seller's market. There aren't any rules here, you just have to learn to trust your instinct, and the more you work in your market, the sharper your instincts will become. Flip through the photos of each listing and let your unconscious mind absorb as much data as possible. Then look for several of the closest comparables in the three main categories of active, pending, and sold until your gut tells you the data look right. That will give you the ballpark figure you need before the appointment.

To double-check, look at expired and withdrawn listings to see if there were any unusual trends. The last step is to widen your search for only active listings and see how your ballpark price would look against the competition if the property were listed today.

That doesn't sound so complicated does it?

I didn't describe adjustments because you rarely need to worry about them. Leave that level of detail for the appraiser. You know what else you don't need to worry about? The app you use for your pricing presentation. I promise you the seller won't care if you talk about price with the latest app or with printed forms.

As I suggested earlier, once you learn to have a high-level pricing discussion, sellers sometimes won't care if you show them any comps. The market analysis has two basic functions:

to help you form your opinion of value, which you may change once you get to the property, and to provide a starting place for the discussion with the seller. So if it's possible you may change your opinion of value during the discussion, it would be a huge waste of time to spend hours on a so-called scientific market analysis.

Experienced agents will tell you that once you get to the appointment, you could discover many factors that alter your opinion. For example, you could learn their idea of "updated" is the kitchen remodel they did fifteen years ago. Or you could discover that one spouse is pushing to get out of the house much faster than the one you spoke to when setting up the appointment.

If the market analysis is simply your opinion, if it's merely a starting point for a discussion and if it's possible you may change your opinion, then clearly we need a fresh way to look at this part of the appointment.

True market value is established the moment buyer and seller agree on a contract price, and immediately after closing, that established value begins to change. So the goal of the pricing presentation is to lead the seller to a place where they pick the right starting price. To be able to do that, you need to know when they want their money. Successful sellers are the ones who pick the right initial listing price. It's not that people who try a higher price, then reduce if they don't get an offer, never sell. But they often get a lower price than if they started at the right price to begin with.

Beyond that, overpriced listings are really bad for business. In every market, there seems to be at least one company known for buying the listing with price. When an agent buys a listing with price, they take the listing at whatever price the seller wants, even when they know the price is too high, because they are just going to wear them down with price reduction requests until they find a buyer. It's an expensive, inefficient, stressful, and, some would argue, unethical way to practice real estate.

The way to lead sellers toward success faster is to help them understand their price is directly related to time. No matter what your opinion of value is and, for that matter, no matter what their opinion is, what they can get for their home is determined by timing.

If they are in no rush, they should be able to extract maximum market value, but the faster they need out, the lower the price will have to be. This is hard for sellers to accept, and it's complicated by the fact that CMAs have never done a good job showing this. In many cases, the more data you give a seller, the more likely they are to get confused. When people are confused or uncertain, they hesitate, and your likelihood of getting a listing will plummet.

Because we're all drowning in information, we need opinions, interpretations, and guidance more than ever. One easy way to help sellers understand the connection between their asking price and time is to move away from real estate and talk about another type of product.

Automobiles prove an easy analogy for everyone to wrap their mind around. Everyone understands that whether the dealer likes it or not, next year's model is coming. One day dealers "want to" sell the cars they already have, the next day they are put under timing pressure and "have to" sell them faster. When that happens, we see commercials with lowered prices and blockbuster deals. Some of us even wait for that exact time to buy and get a deal.

Discussions like this help the seller reframe their property from a home to a product and helping the seller see their home as a product like any other is one of the best ways to guide them toward picking the right starting price.

The CMA Goal: Get to the Net

The fastest and easiest way to guide a seller to the right initial listing price is counterintuitive. That's because instead of focusing on the asking price, the goal is to focus on net proceeds. The net is the only number a seller really cares about anyway, but because most people aren't versed like you are in doing a net sheet, they only know how to discuss the issue in terms of asking price.

The same is true for your competition. While every other agent wrestles over the price with the seller, you have another chance to set yourself apart. Therefore, the method you use to frame this discussion in terms of net depends on how much price agreement you have with the seller. Here are three options. (Note: As you work with these pricing methodologies, it's important to understand you must always be prepared with your market analysis just in case you need to fall back on it. Also, some states and/or brokers require you deliver a formal CMA to the seller on a listing appointment. If that's the case, double-check your specific obligations and, if allowed, do that at the end, after you've agreed the seller is comfortable with the net and you've made your mutual decisions about working together.)

Start with the Net: Occasionally, you and the seller will be in agreement on price right away. If you don't discover a situation on the appointment that would cause you to adjust, like condition or timing, simply tell them you agree and suggest looking at what they'd likely walk away with at closing. In other words, just skip to the net.

Remember, too much detail confuses people and can be counterproductive for both you and the seller. This is going to feel strange at first because most agents are conditioned to believe that presenting a CMA is the one and only way to discuss price. But I lost count over the years of how much time I saved when I was released from the sense of obligation of poring over the detail in a CMA when sometimes they didn't even want to see it.

If you've built up trust with the seller and they are happy with the estimated net, they'll often be happy moving forward to the next step to discuss disclosures and listing agreements.

Narrow the Gap: More often, their opinion of price and yours will differ, but the gap isn't extreme. When you feel you need to guide the seller down a bit to maximize their chances of getting the highest price possible within their desired time frame, you can ask a series of questions to narrow the gap. For example, ask:

- What if you couldn't get $500,000? What would you do?
- I'm just curious what you would do if you couldn't get $500,000. Would you cancel your plans altogether?
- What if all you could get is $489,000? I'm not saying you'd be thrilled, but if you walked away from closing with enough cash, would you even consider it?
- Would you like to see an estimate of how much cash you'd walk away with at closing if you sold at that price?

And just like that, you've moved off of price and onto net proceeds. You see, often sellers who start off being stuck on one certain price let go of attachment to it once you show them that at a lower price they will still have enough cash to make their move. So many agents make the mistake of assuming that getting every single dollar out of a home is the most important goal for sellers. Sometimes it is, but more often than not, they're looking to strike a balance. Money on its own is important to people, but using money to realize the vision of their new lifestyle is more important.

In a Pickle: Sometimes your opinion of price and the sellers' will be really far apart. Don't let this intimidate you. You can learn to show up ready to handle a seller who is way out of the ballpark, and once you realize how simple it is, any stress you hold around working with sellers on price will fall away.

When you're far apart on opinion of price, you have two basic options. You could show them your opinion and then try to talk them into listing at your price, which is what your competition does, or you could persuade them to insist on hearing your honest opinion of the right initial listing price.

I call this method "in a pickle" because of the trial close you used as you transitioned from your solution selling–based marketing presentation into the pricing discussion. In fact, your ability to use this method depends on your use of that trial close. So you don't have to look back, the trial close is, "Assuming we can agree on price, would anything stop you from hiring me tonight?"

Now here's the pickle that puts you in: You could just agree to start at their price and walk out with a new listing because they've already told you they'd hire you if you agree. That's a super exciting and highly addictive feeling. But it's short-lived because you know that as soon as you wake up the next day, you're going to begin to stress over how to get that first price reduction. Or you could tell them what you really think about price and risk walking away with no listing because you couldn't agree.

In other words, the pickle you are in is to tell them what they need to hear or what they want to hear. Obviously, you want to tell them what they need to hear, but the trick is to make it their idea. In order to do that, simply paint a picture of how you got to this place. Describe how you took all the information from the initial call and did your research to support the price they told you they wanted. Describe how you combed through every piece of data you could find and how you talked about their house with other agents when you couldn't find any data to support what they wanted. Explain how no matter where you looked or to whom you spoke, you just couldn't find any way to support their asking price.

This is exactly what plays out every day in offices across the country. And as you describe all of this, they think you are in a pickle because you can't justify their price. But that can't be the reason because no individual person is able to influence a market. The data are what they are, and you merely report what you find. So after you paint this picture, remind them they told you they'd hire you if you agreed on the price and ask them to make a choice. On matters this important in their life, ask if they would rather you tell them what they want to hear or what they need to hear.

That is a powerful question, and although they may joke, I can't ever remember a person declining to hear what they needed to hear. So no matter how far apart you are, now is the time to hit them with whatever the right price is based on your research. Then when they hear it, as fast as you can, acknowledge you understand it can be a shock and suggest that before they make decisions, they take a look at what they'd walk away with at closing. And now, in a healthy and respectful way, you've had an honest conversation about price and you are talking about what they really care about—the net.

Did you notice? Still no discussion of the details of a CMA. But if there was a time your seller might ask to cover the data in more detail, this is commonly when it happens, and, yes, you do have to be prepared to show them your research. When you do, start with the summary and very cautiously back into the data. Use only the amount of detail you need to help them see you really aren't trying to pull a fast one.

Converting to Net

Now you have three unique ways to deliver your pricing presentation that minimize the risk of confusing the seller by overwhelming them with too much data. You've also avoided the scenario where too much weight is put on the value of each individual comparable home. That means your potential client should have the bandwidth left to absorb the information on the estimate of net proceeds.

This is one area where it's good to go into detail. Because net proceeds calculations aren't that complicated, it's really hard to overwhelm people. This is an important part of the closing process so it should never be skipped. Once you've done the net sheet and worked down to the bottom line, the key to more signatures and higher conversion rates is to move forward assumptively.

The next item on your listing appointment agenda then is to talk about your forms. The best way to transition to that discussion is to simply ask if they have any questions on how you determined the net estimate. It's common to see a seller in deep thought at this moment. As they are mentally preparing for a decision, they will often become more serious and thoughtful. You'll see and feel this energy. Often, their face will become more focused, their responses will become shorter, and they'll lean into the table. These are all good signs, and it's really important you don't talk so much that you interrupt their decision-making process. The process you're working with provides the space for them to do this so it's your job to remain calm and gently lead them forward.

Forms and Disclosures

If no one has ever said this to you, I need to: you must read your forms regularly. I mean, read them for understanding so you have a grasp on what each paragraph means, not just what it says. The better your understanding of the forms your state requires you to use, the easier this part of the process will be. Because most of the forms used in real estate are promulgated by the state, your clients won't likely feel the need to read every word if you explain what they'll be signing for general understanding.

Of course, it's an incredibly smart business practice to offer them the opportunity to sit there and read through word for word any or all of it if they would like. After you've covered the forms and disclosures, move forward assumptively again by asking if they have any questions.

Getting the Signature

I find this exact moment of the appointment fascinating, and it's also thrilling. Both you and the sellers will likely experience an adrenaline rush. As long as they grunt when you ask if they have any questions, I want you to hand them the pen, tell them where to sign (or how if you're working on a tablet), and then I want you to break direct eye contact. Grab your bag and other items you've used during your appointment and start packing up.

When you do this, you are sending the signal nonverbally that you're done. All they have to do is sign and then everyone can move on with their day. The last step of your agenda, the mutual decision, is implied.

If by that point you had determined you didn't want the listing, you wouldn't be offering your services officially by asking them to sign. And if they decide they don't want to hire you, they won't sign. The reason you need to break direct eye contact is because people need a private moment to commit. And if you're with a couple, sometimes they need that moment to signal to each other that they are in agreement to move forward. They can't do that if you're all up in their grill.

Are you married, or have you ever been, or even in a close relationship for a while? Then I bet you can have robust conversations with your partner and never say a word. You just give them "that look" right?

Because of the energy rush of this moment, it's important to make sure you don't get carried away and blow it. When you hand them the pen or tablet and ask them to sign, even though you've looked away, you'll still sense what's going on. Sometimes what's going on is a lot of wiggling and not much talking. Traditionally, that wiggling in silence makes salespeople super nervous. Have you ever heard a sales trainer say, once you ask for a signature, whoever speaks next loses? Well, there's a bit of truth to that, so it's really important not to let your nerves get the best of you. Understanding the yes monster will help you keep them under control.

The Yes Monster

Picture a seller wiggling in silence at the kitchen table with the pen in their hand. The wiggling is the yes monster trying to get out.

Think of the last time you made a big decision that made you nervous. Maybe it was when you bought your last car. Right before you signed the purchase agreement, there was likely a flood of thoughts that went through your mind where you asked yourself one final time if you're really doing this. Your fears and doubts likely made one last attempt before you beat them back and moved forward with what you really wanted to do. All of that energy is what causes the wiggling.

If you can discipline yourself to just remain calm and quiet and not engage them directly, the yes monster will find his way out. The yes monster is very strong and will eventually win. This is because people always do what they feel like doing. You know the yes monster has escaped when you notice out of the corner of your eye they are signing. Sometimes you can hear the pen scratching across the paper.

The moment the seller makes the decision, the energy shifts. You are now officially a team and everyone will feel a massive release of positive energy. But never forget, if you keep talking because you're nervous, the yes monster will give up and go back to sleep.

Of course, the yes monster doesn't always win that easily. Sometimes he cries out for help. If he needs help, you'll hear what you think is an objection, but it's actually something else. That's what I cover next.

In my opinion, this is the most creative part of the sales process. If you think about the four parts: take control, find the problem, solve the problem, and close, nothing comes after close. Then, if you think about how we took those four steps and built an appointment agenda around them, ending with a mutual decision, nothing comes after the decision. Objections aren't directly mentioned and that's one of your clues to deeper understanding. Making a mutual decision implies there is going to be an agreement to move forward or not. An objection is neither.

The main objective on all of your appointments is to get a yes or a no. You are far better off with one of the two than with a maybe that will never materialize. Maybes are safe ground for adults because they allow us to avoid making decisions. Saying yes is very final. Saying no is also very final. Maybe is so safe because it gets us out of a yes that we might later regret and a no that we feel uncomfortable stating.

But make no mistake, it's the maybes that will kill you in sales, and every time you leave a listing appointment with no decision, you're stuck as a prisoner of hope. When you go back to the office or home, the first question people ask is if you got the business and you're left expressing hope that the seller will call you back. Here's the hard truth; they are not going to call you back. I know many of you will have that one time a seller called you back, but we all know that's the exception, not the rule.

When living as a prisoner of hope, you make follow-up calls that don't get answered, or when they do, the decision is put off further. You check the MLS every day to see if the listing was lost to another firm. Each follow-up call is a bit more demoralizing and leaves many feeling like a salesperson chasing down business. Sadly, this adds up to huge amounts of lost productivity time because the average agent hangs way too much on each appointment.

If listing appointments are few and far between, it's easy to get attached and lose sleep while you wait for the seller's decision. Some agents literally become frozen and don't even realize they've stopped all lead generating activity until they find out what a seller is going to do. This isn't conscious behavior and that makes it even more dangerous.

The good news is you're here and about to learn a better way. We're going to speed all this up. After all, the whole point of improving sales methodologies is to go on more appointments and get more decisions, faster. But first, you must resolve that you deserve a yes or a no on your appointments. After all the work you put in to help the sellers, the least they can do is be honest with you and make a decision.

Advancements, Continuances, and Objections

Broadly speaking, when you're working with people in any sales process, you can get one of three outcomes at each stage: an advancement, a continuance, or an objection. An advancement is a clear, affirmative decision or commitment to take future action. Advancements are always good. When you are lead generating, an example of an advancement would be a scheduled appointment. On a listing appointment, an advancement is a signed agreement. And when parties are negotiating a sales agreement, advancements are any concessions and agreements that lead to the executed contract.

A continuance, on the other hand, is an absence of a commitment to take any future action other than following up. It's when they punt the ball by telling you they want to think about it. In other words, it's not a yes or a no and it puts you into a follow-up loop. Continuances aren't the end of the world because, if you are getting them, it means that at least you are active in the marketplace. Following up is a normal part of business, but once you're on the appointment itself, you should use every skill you have to avoid a continuance. Remember, they don't call you back.

In the context of a listing appointment, a continuance is simply a cover-up. It's what they say that obscures the real reason they aren't making a decision. You could even say a stall is a lie. Not a malicious lie but in any case it's not the truth and not the full story.

When you get a continuance, here's what you can know for sure: there is something bothering them that they feel uncomfortable telling you. Their reasons are not always going to make sense because all of this comes from emotion, not logic. The classic continuance is, "We want to think it over." But when you leave, they aren't thinking about anything. They aren't sleeping on it or reviewing your presentation, and they certainly aren't praying about it. No, as soon as you leave, they start talking. More specifically, they start talking about the actual reason they didn't move forward with you. When top producers get a continuance, their number one goal is to discover the real objection.

The objection is the actual reason a person isn't moving forward in the moment. It's the reason you must uncover if you hope to have any chance of advancement. Objections are clear issues that can be addressed. For example, "We want to talk to other agents first" is an objection. So is, "We are looking for an agent with a lower fee" and "We would like to try to sell it ourselves first."

Specific and defined statements like that are actual objections and objections *can* be handled. When people give you an objection, they are trying to tell you they are either scared, need some space, or need help understanding a specific topic. Consider someone whose objection is that they want to speak to other agents before they decide which one to hire. Odds are they fear not doing enough research and feel like they need time to weigh their options.

Have you ever put off a decision for fear of making a mistake only to end up more confused and unsure after you've done all your research? That could happen to the seller, so the process for overcoming objections is designed to help them alleviate fears and provide the space necessary for them to become comfortable with a decision. Except you don't have to leave and wait for them to call back for that to happen.

Digging out the real objection isn't that hard once you're aware that "thinking about it" isn't an objection. Sometimes if you just ask people what's holding them back, they will tell you. In real estate it turns out there are common sets of reasons people are hesitating, and you can start by literally going down the list. They might be concerned about the (1) price you suggested and are afraid to say so or, closely connected to that reason, they were hoping the (2) net proceeds would be higher. There could be terms in your (3) listing agreement bothering them or they could be concerned about either (4) you or your (5) company.

Ask the seller, one by one, if any of those five areas are bothering them and encourage them to expand.

If you get through all of those five subjects and they don't express what's really on their mind, you can repackage them. People generally have issues with money, timing, or trusting others. If a seller is still being cagey after you've inquired about the five subjects and more, just repackage the way you are asking them. Let them know you don't think they should hire anyone unless they are sure the net looks acceptable, that now is the time for them to move, and that they feel they can trust you. After expressing that, look them straight in the eye and ask which of those three is bothering them.

This is basically asking the same questions you did before in a different way, and in my experience, it almost always flushed out the real objection. "Well, I'll tell you, Jasen. We trust you, but the agent we met last night said we could ask $10,000 more, and we could really use that money." Bingo. That's a real objection (money), and now you can work to overcome it.

Objection Handling Track

When a top producer uncovers a real objection, they use a time-tested process to create space for the seller to make a decision. Nearly everyone else will simply try to talk a person into signing an agreement, if they make any attempt at all.

Unless you are carrying a gun (and are foolish), you aren't going to be able to say anything to force a seller to do what they don't want to do. If you use the objection handling track and they sign your agreement, it means they wanted to do it and you were able to make them feel safe doing so.

This is a wonderful service to provide for another person and should help free your mind from concern about being seen as pushy. Top producers never even ponder the word *pushy*. There just isn't time to indulge in those thoughts of the ego because they've learned to put their focus squarely on the client's interest and trust their objection handling track to do the work.

The objection handling track has six steps:

1. Validate them
2. Question with curiosity
3. Compartmentalize
4. Get a commitment
5. Solve with a visual
6. Close

Validate Them: When you hear the real objection, first make a statement that signals you aren't going to put up a fight. When a person tells you what's really bothering them, they instantly put up defenses as they mentally prepare to defend their position, and you simply can't work with them while their defenses are up. Before people can be persuaded, they must feel as if they have been heard, and when they do, it gives you a small opening to move forward. A simple way to do this would be to nod your head and say, "I hear you. No problem."

Question with Curiosity: The next step is to begin to question their position with curiosity. Once again, channel your inner five-year-old and work to get to the root of why they feel the way they feel. If you simply ask why they feel the way they do, you can get them talking. This is critical because talking is one way humans relieve tension. The more you can get them to talk and expand on their reasons, the easier it'll be to work with them.

You must remember, however, not to insert your opinions at this point. Your only goal here is to get them to open up and talk. As they explain what's on their mind, jot down what they say in case there are multiple concerns. Often you'll find there's just one or maybe two items they want to address.

Compartmentalize: Once you've sensed they've expressed their major concerns, test it by compartmentalizing those concerns and feeding them back to the seller. That means repeating what they told you and asking if there's anything you missed or if that's it. What you're doing here is demonstrating that you are working to understand them. For example, "I heard you say _____. Is there anything else on your mind?"

Get a Commitment: You get a commitment by using a trial close. In this case the best one is this: "If I could _____, would you _____?" What you're doing here is asking if you could put their mind at ease, would they hire you now? The first few times you ask this, it'll feel extremely gutsy. But eventually, it'll become standard operating procedure.

Solve with a Visual: Often from the moment you hear the real objection, you'll be compelled to respond. But as you can see, the track forces you to hold back until the appropriate time. Now that you have had a chance to ensure the seller feels heard and, even better, understood, you are free to share why you think they should move forward now. This is where you'll use sales magnets to obtain signatures. As a reminder, sales magnets are just ideas, reduced to visuals, given names, and used to persuade people. Initially I discussed them in the context of getting appointments, and they work just the same to get more signatures.

The hardest part for agents initially is getting in the habit of using their creativity to come up with a variety of sales magnets. Even though I discussed this before during the conversion chain, it's going to be helpful to look at an example for use on a listing appointment where you need to persuade someone to overcome an objection.

Many years ago, my stepmother told me in February she'd like to sell her home. This was a big deal because it's the home she owned with my deceased father and, as you can imagine, selling came with tons of emotion. After looking at the market in the neighborhood, I learned that inventory was really low and every home that was listed was receiving multiple offers. Even so, she wanted to wait until the spring. The reason was simply "because that's when you sell homes." She did in fact wait.

By spring, it turned out that everyone else in the neighborhood was thinking along the same lines. Every metric showed the broader market was as healthy as it could get, except one. Instead of two other homes for sale in the area, there were now over forty. How could anyone have seen that coming? There was no way to know that all of these families were going to decide to move at the same time. In the end, the house sold for thousands of dollars less than it would have just a few months earlier.

Now, how would you take that situation and create a sales magnet? Got any ideas? I'm going to help you here, but as you move through your career, the challenge will be for you to develop the ability to do this for yourself and build up your library.

Here's the idea: Create a custom map on Google and mark the houses that were for sale in February. Next, ask the listing agents how many offers were received. Take the number of offers and the percentage above asking price received and include it on the map. Then create another layer on the map and do the same for May's listings and call it the seller group-think case study. In the notes you could include some of the broader economic numbers that showed a healthy market overall.

With a visual like that, you could literally show a seller who wanted to wait a real example of other sellers who got caught in a micro buyer's market through no fault of their own. Now it may not happen to these sellers in this neighborhood but that's not the point. The point is that events like that do happen, out of the blue, and when they do, the seller loses.

Top producers aren't in business to paint best-case scenarios for their clients, especially if they want happy clients. The best way to serve all of your clients is to help them make decisions by understanding worst-case scenarios. We know that rarely happens, but if it does, at least you will have prepared them.

Here's a big key to this whole process: after you show them your visual and explain it, you must assume that anyone who sees it will have been persuaded. That assumption leads you right into the close.

Close: "So, Mr. and Mrs. Seller, when you look at it that way, it would be crazy to wait any longer wouldn't it." There is a period at the end of the sentence because I don't want you to ask it with the tone of a question. Rather, picture yourself with all the confidence you can muster, looking the seller straight in the eye and vocalizing that question as more of a matter-of-fact statement.

Read it again and say it like that in your mind. Okay, do it again, and this time, as you do, gently nod your head up and down in a yes motion. Now you're using all of your elements of persuasive presenting. You used their name, asked a question with the appropriate tone, and used a visual. This is masterful persuasion at its best.

Do you remember the yes monster who causes the wiggles inside a seller when you ask a question? Well, if the seller successfully held that monster down before and gave you the objection you're now handling, this process provides all the opening the yes monster needs to attempt another escape. After you deliver that line, hand them the pen once more signaling it's time to wrap up. If they sign the agreement, congratulations. It means you have created the space necessary for them to feel safe.

One well-executed run through the objection handling track is almost all you'll ever need to dramatically increase your conversion rates on listing appointments. However, there will be times when you will hear another objection.

Just like I guided you to close three times for an appointment, the same guidance applies here. There is no way you can allow yourself to come this far and then give up after handling one objection. I'm not saying you have to handle ten, but definitely as many as three if needed. What this means is that you'll need a minimum of three sales magnets available for use at all times.

When doing live workshops, I'll often have the group list the most common objections they receive and then build a list of possible sales magnets to overcome them. Once we have those two lists, we'll go further and write descriptions of what they will do for the seller. An exercise like this is so effective because you'll only close for the signature in relation to how many sales magnets you have.

Let me explain. If you only have two that you truly understand, you'll only close two times on any given appointment. To help you begin building your own sales magnet library, I've included the exercise I do in live workshops along with common magnets in the website bonus. [You can find all website bonuses at jasenedwards.com/TPLBonus.]

Here's an extreme example of handling objections:

One day I was prospecting For Sale By Owners, and I scheduled an appointment with a nice woman named Jean who promised her husband, Rod, would be there. Once I got there, it wasn't long before I learned they had just been on the market with another agent for six months. They put the FSBO sign in their yard after the listing expired. So was I on an appointment with a FSBO or an expired listing? The crazy answer is both. For some reason that was the first time I'd even considered that some FSBOs may have been listed before. It was my longest appointment ever, clocking in at over five hours. Between the sales magnets I'd built for use with FSBOs and expired listings, I easily had more than ten from which to choose. I don't remember how many of them I used, but I think it was all of them, and I'm sure I had to make some up on the fly toward the end of the appointment.

I remember being extremely uncomfortable because, while I had a strong commitment to close three times in all cases, I was also committed to not going past three. Some schools of thought say you should close until you get it. Not only was I not mentored that way, it just never felt right to me. But I joke that Jean certainly subscribed to the idea of closing until you get it because every time I'd use a sales magnet and close for the signature, her husband would give me another objection. That would trigger a look from Jean that I can only describe as "young man if you leave I will track you down."

Honestly, those looks from Jean scared me more than the times Rod got up and paced the floor in front of his gun cabinet. I'm not even kidding about that. So somewhere along the line after more than five hours and the use of every visual I had (and was able to create on the fly), Rod signed the listing agreement at the price I suggested and at full commission.

My biggest lesson? Follow the wife's lead. All kidding aside, the real lesson was to let the track provide the space to do its work. Looking back, Rod always wanted to hire me. He just needed a ton of space (over five hours apparently) to get there. I never had another appointment like that, and to this day I believe it happened to me so that I could write about it here and anchor the importance of this work we do.

Most agents would get frustrated with Rod and leave, which meant he and Jean would have been left to navigate the sale on their own. Neither of them wanted to do that. Rod had a lot of emotion going on inside and needed a professional who was able to hold space for him to work through all of it. Hanging in there and working through a situation any other agent would have given up on after maybe ninety minutes led to business from several of their family members. Now, more than twenty years later, I still have the wind chimes Rod made me as a closing gift. Cool, huh?

When it comes to closing three times, I want you to remember to be committed to the methodology but also kind to yourself. When I was learning to close three times, the first big challenge was doing so while scheduling appointments, and I had to overcome all of the fears and emotions that everyone else faces. This is your race and you aren't in competition with anyone else.

When I say be kind to yourself, I mean don't compare yourself to others who may seem to have it all figured out. I promise you they don't. Stay committed to closing three times and allow yourself to grow at whatever pace works for you. One day, you'll end a call with a fantastic appointment on your calendar and realize after the fact that you closed three times to get that appointment. When it happens, drop me a line and let me know about it. I would love to celebrate with you.

The same goes for closing three times for the signature. Getting skilled at closing on the phone doesn't always translate to being good at it in person. It's amazing how adjusting the context slightly makes a huge difference. It's the same methodology at work, but in a different setting; closing requires another level of learning and growth.

One day, you'll drive away from a property with a newly signed listing agreement and a tremendous rush of energy because you hung in there and asked that third time for the signature. Because you trusted the methodology, you have a new client and are providing for your family. I want to hear from you when this happens, too, because at this point, it'll be about so much more than the money.

The commissions are nice, but when you've controlled the appointment from beginning to end, persuaded the seller to list at the right price, closed three times for the signature, and driven away with a key to the house, you'll have gained something money can't ever buy: confidence in yourself.

You won't walk through the office the next day, you'll strut. Then you'll realize, if you can do that once, you can do it again, and again and again until you've helped enough people to build the life you dreamed of when you got your license. Very few people ever make it to this place in real estate. When you do, a celebration is in order. A celebration of the Top Producer Life.

Fun Money

One last strategy I want to share with you before we move on is what you can do if you close three times on an appointment and you still don't get a signature.

As I mentioned, I'm not a big believer in the idea that you should close until you get the listing. I feel you can damage relationships that way. So when you close that third time and still don't get a signature, it's time to let go. You did your best and, to be sure, far more than any other agent would have done, so give yourself credit for that and move on.

The majority of the time, when you leave the appointment without the signature, you aren't getting the listing—ever. They'll sound so sincere when they tell you they'll call you back, but listen to me when I say this, they won't. So let them go and move on to your next appointment. Put them on your long-term marketing plan if you want and don't even bother calling them back to see if they've made a decision. Most likely they've already decided and the decision was that they aren't hiring you.

Sometimes no matter what you do or say, people just won't come out and tell you they aren't interested. It's like that *Sex and the City* episode where Carrie's boyfriend Berger tells Miranda that "when a guy says he'll call but doesn't, he's just not that into you." If you remember that episode, you'll know what a relief that was for Miranda. When she knew what was really going on, she was free to let go too.

Some sellers just won't be that into you. But what if occasionally they do call back? There's one of you out there thinking about the time someone called you back to list their home. I know, that happened to me too. It's just so rare that it's not worth obsessing over. Because I wasn't walking around a prisoner of hope waiting for their decision, I wasn't counting on that commission. I learned quickly how much easier it is to let go and get on with my life and business.

So I started playing a game we called fun money in my house. Anytime I left an appointment without a signature, I'd write the address on a whiteboard in the kitchen. No one ever counted on these addresses ever turning into business, but on the odd occasion they did, the commission earned became fun money, and we'd blow it on a trip, furniture, or sometimes just an extravagant night out. As long as it wasn't a bill. The whole point was to be irresponsible with fun money!

Working with Buyers: How to Sell More Houses with Fewer Showings

I'm going to start by telling you that buyers were never my favorite type of client. Almost immediately I could tell that top producers focused on listings, and in the early days of my career I didn't know why. I just knew I wanted to be a top producer so I developed an early preference for listings.

Initially, listings were a huge mystery to me. Before I learned the strategies you just read, I did what nearly everyone else who gets into the business does: I started looking for buyers. In those days, we'd sign up a month in advance at a sales meeting for an activity called phone duty where we'd take turns sitting in a little room for a few hours next to the receptionist answering the calls that came in from yard signs and other ads. Phone duty was one big way agents who didn't have listings got leads, and even though it's rare to see an actual phone duty room in a real estate office these days, some agents still look for a company who promises to provide the most leads.

However, the majority of the advertising placed to generate buyer leads in real estate uses listings because they are the fastest way to a steady stream of leads. Sometimes I'll be asked how to get buyers in a particular area, like a higher-dollar area or a popular part of town. The answer is to focus not on buyers but on listings in those areas. Do that and guess who starts to show up? Buyers who are looking in and who can afford those areas.

At this point, you probably knew I was going to say that. Chasing buyers is never a good activity to find yourself doing, but you will see it happening all around you. Typically, when an agent is under financial pressure and needs a commission quickly, all attention turns to finding a buyer. It's easy to understand why.

How many times have you heard a story of another agent who connected with a buyer at an open house, showed them property the next day, and by the end of the week had them under contract with a thirty-day close? Agents hear stories like that enough to make them think that turning a buyer is the fastest way to generate income. Of course, those stories conveniently leave out all of the other buyers who have been kicking tires for nine months while the agent drives them all over creation pulling her hair out.

Also, listings require an initial outlay of cash to advertise, which seems too risky or not possible for someone who is just starting or who hasn't had a sale in several months. When you don't have the skills to schedule a listing appointment and convert a seller into a paying client, it's tempting to meet a buyer at a home, unlock the door, and show them around. Fingers crossed on this one, right?

One of my first buyer clients was Beth, a hairdresser who wanted to buy her first home. At the time, I had no listings and my sales skills were nonexistent. That meant we didn't have any kind of buyer consultation and I certainly didn't have a signed buyer representation agreement. I'd like to think I was smart enough to have an agency disclosure signed but who knows. I was terrified to ask anyone to sign agreements and disclosures, even if the law required it.

So one day Beth found a house she wanted to see thirty

minutes from my office. After my phone duty shift, I drove all the way down there to open it up. She loved it and we made an offer that day. I was on a massive high and loving life. Then came the inspection and, right after that, word came from the lender that he wasn't going to be able to get the loan through underwriting because of the way she recorded her income as a hairstylist.

Beth needed to get out of her contract, and I had just lost a sale. It was the first time I understood this roller coaster people would always mention. It was a financial and emotional roller coaster. I was sick to my stomach, and the failed sale left such an impression on me that I can still remember driving to the office to call the listing agent and tell her the deal was off. I called from the car because I was too embarrassed to make the call from the office where others could hear.

I'll also never forget her response: "No problem. This happens and we'll find another buyer." Really? How could she not be devastated? That made me want to have listings even more, but I knew I wasn't going to be able to escape buyers completely so I had to figure this out.

STRAIGHTEN OUT THE CONFUSION WITH BUYERS

The three tests: It only takes a few times getting burned to realize you've spent way too much time working with someone who is never going to buy to start setting some standards for yourself. You've probably heard that saying "buyers are liars." I don't buy that so much as I do the fact that too many agents show houses to people they shouldn't. "Buyers are liars" is the wrong lesson to take away from the times you've lost a buyer one way or another.

The two more painful, but also more valuable lessons are (1) when we fail to set standards, we end up showing homes to people who are lookers not buyers, and (2) when we fail to widen the search, we aren't creating enough space for the buyer to discover what they really want.

The rule of thumb is to follow up with lookers and chain yourself to the buyers. To make sure you are working with people who are ready, willing, and able to purchase, they should have to pass three tests:

▶ Test 1: They are willing to meet you in your office (your meeting space) having done their homework with a lender.

▶ Test 2: They open up and freely share their thoughts during your initial consultation.

▶ Test 3: They sign your buyer's representation agreement and state they'd be willing to make an offer whenever it is they find the right home. Day one or day twenty-one.

TEXT TO TALK TO TABLE TO TERMS

Remember the conversion chain? It's every bit as important to use when working with buyers.

When people are under stress, their behavior isn't always rational. The conversion chain tells us that before we show property to a buyer, we need to convert them to an appointment (get them to the table) and then to a client we officially represent (terms). When you short-cut this process and work with buyers in a random fashion, it confuses them and, frankly, hurts the profession.

The conversion chain will help you weed through the tire kickers faster, convert more of your buyer leads into appointments, and sell houses to more of those buyers. This is critical to the long-term health of your practice because everyone knows working with listings is far more leveraged. When you take a listing, you and every other agent in your market gets to work together to find the buyer.

But when you work buyers, it's just you and them. The more efficient you are with your buyers, the more time you'll have to spend on building your listing inventory. This starts with a commitment to work with buyers who are willing to meet you and follow up with those who won't. More specifically, it means you must set a standard for your business that you don't show houses to people whom you don't officially represent in writing.

It won't be a problem for you to hold that standard once you begin to think bigger than just opening doors and walking people through transactions. Buyers take an emotional journey just like sellers do, and if you don't stay on track, you can end up confusing them.

There was a time when I needed the help of an intellectual property attorney. When I met in his office for the initial consultation, there was some small talk followed by lots of questions. The attorney wanted to know what I was trying to accomplish and why. After he felt he understood, he decided he could help and explained how he worked. This included an overview of how he thought the project would play out, an estimate of how much time it would take, and what he thought the total cost would be based on the firm's fee structure. Then he presented me with a few disclosures and an agreement to hire them.

If that sounds similar to the listing appointment process we covered, then I know you're learning fast. But imagine if instead of leading me through a professional appointment, the attorney offered to email me a couple different options for free while I thought about it. What if every few days he sent me different ways I could work toward my objective of protecting the intellectual property? Imagine him calling me and asking this: Did you look at that strategy that I sent? What did you think? Would you like to see more options? When you decide on one I can help you through the whole process. Are you talking to any other attorneys? Pick me. Pick me.

That sounds ridiculous doesn't it. And agents do this all the time. When any service professional fails to lead a prospect through a professional appointment, they inadvertently confuse the client. If an attorney keeps giving me free information and never shows me how to become a client, I end up thinking he's a nice person, but I'm not likely to ever say, "Please send me a contract so I can hire you." Why would I if I keep getting free stuff?

More importantly, that's not my role as the customer; it's the responsibility of the professional to ask for the business. Likewise, when agents spend huge amounts of time emailing properties to people and showing them house after house for free without asking them for any direct commitment, the buyers end up thinking the agent is a really nice person but don't afford them any professional respect.

Have you ever busted your butt to find a buyer the exact home they described only to be continually frustrated because you can get close, but never exactly what the buyer says they want? Then one day, it magically appears, but the buyer, who never signed a buyer rep agreement, has gone cold.

Finally you reach them and after an enthusiastic description of the property, there is a long pause, followed by a confession that they found a house two weeks ago. Wait, what? How? You looked every day and this is the first time a home like they described was listed. But it's too late. The home they bought was in a totally different part of town, smaller than they insisted on, and $50,000 more than they said they could afford. Then you say that same lie we all have: "Oh, I'm so happy for you." Ugh.

You see, the problem is they were never shown how to become a client. While you were busy giving away all this free information, which they could get on their own online anyway, they tripped upon a property to which they had an emotional reaction. You didn't send it to them because it didn't fit the narrow parameters of your search. The listing sold itself to them, as we say.

Although you're a nice person, when they were in the open house, the listing agent told them there were other interested buyers and they had to act fast. Or so they thought. Again, there is no logic here. Buyers buy based on emotion, and it's our job as professionals to understand that buyers never know what they want until they walk into it. It's fine to start with a general list of features, but buyers will always buy the home they react to emotionally, and there is simply no way of knowing in advance which property will trigger that response.

Therefore, if you don't want this to happen to you, or if you're tired of this happening to you, the first step is to show your buyer prospects how to become clients by drawing them to the line. It's the same process we worked on with sellers, but for some reason, when you hear it this way with buyers in mind, it'll sink in faster.

SALES MAGNETS FOR BUYERS

Meeting a buyer at a home before they are actually your client is not only dangerous (some agents, often females, have met danger and even death meeting with an unknown "buyer"), but confusing for the buyer and causes tons of wasted time in the form of continuances and follow-up loops.

The solution is to commit to learning how to schedule a proper consultation.

When buyers enter the marketplace, they bump around agents until they find one who's got the skill to stop them and schedule an appointment. You know the game Hungry Hippos? That's how I think of agents and buyer leads. The little white balls are the buyers, and when they get into the game (the market), they bump around all over the place until one of the hippos is able to catch it. You already know how to do this. I just taught you in the context of a listing so it's going to be easier for you to understand here.

You already know you're only limited by your own imagination when it comes to creating sales magnets. Buyers are just as busy as sellers, so before they give you some of their time, you'll need an offer compelling enough for them to meet you under favorable conditions. To schedule appointments with buyers, your offer to meet needs to be more compelling than the listing they've found. I'm sure over time you'll have your own robust library of sales magnets for your buyer leads, but I want to cover one with you that has worked best for me and most of my students over the years. It's timeless and highly addictive—even more so than any house they could find on their own.

HIDDEN PROPERTY, GOOD DEALS, AND LEFTOVERS

What can you really offer a buyer for their time? What do you have that is unique to you and more enticing than the home they just found online? Primarily, access.

Every day in real estate offices and online groups, agents talk about properties they have coming soon. As they describe these properties, another agent identifies one of their buyer clients who has been looking for property just like that. The showing is set up and, bingo, the property goes under contact without ever hitting the open market. This is not a debate on whether skipping the MLS and giving the broader market a chance to compete is bad for the seller.

Frankly, I see agents get so attached to their own opinion on that detail, they forget that it's ultimately the seller's call. Regardless, this happens in every kind of market. It doesn't matter if the economy is thriving or struggling, the prime properties always go first and they always go fast. This means there are properties hidden from the buyer's view if they aren't teamed up with an agent who's plugged in. It means any truly special properties or amazing deals will be gone before the average buyer gets a chance to see them.

In a way, it means properties sitting in the MLS are the leftovers. Can you wrap your mind around that? If you got a listing that was in great shape but the seller needed out fast so they priced it $50,000 below a fair asking price, would you schedule an open house for the public and maybe an expensive brokers open with a catered lunch to see if there'd be any interest? Hell no. You'd squawk about it to your colleagues, and it'd be snatched up before you knew it.

Generally, listings lingering in the MLS are essentially the homes passed over by the buyers already in the market when it was listed. Cold mashed potatoes and green beans. You can warm them up in the microwave by getting a price reduction, but the end result is never as desirable.

Among the various places consumers make purchases,

when are they most conditioned to think they are going to get something really special or a good deal? When they shop retail? Certainly not. The good deals and special finds are always found when we buy direct. Often, buyers look at homes for sale by owner because they perceive they'll be able to get a deal.

I love shoes, and sometimes with my favorite shoemaker, I'm able to buy a really special and unique pair directly from them because the retail stores chose not to carry that specific style. In many ways across many types of products and services, society conditions your future buyer clients to crave deals and special finds. No one wants microwaved mashed potatoes and green beans.

Access, then, is what you have to offer and that's just an idea. Now, to turn access into a usable sales magnet that you can offer to your leads, you need a name and a visual. Think about other industries. When you work with an insider, it's almost always wrapped around some sort of marketing. At Nordstrom you can be in the personal shopper program, and at Apple you can enroll your company in the Apple Business Manager Program. Both offer access to levels of service not readily available to the general public. Even banks have separate divisions where they use terms like *private banking* or *wealth management* as their offer to attract higher net worth clients.

The trick for your sales magnets is to remember you're only limited by your imagination. When someone works directly and exclusively with you to buy a home, what would you call it? Your direct buyer program? Private buyer program? If you notice, brokerages and franchise systems do this to a degree for their luxury divisions, and there is nothing stopping you from implementing your own sales magnets in your individual practice.

It's what buyers of all kinds of services expect after all, and it's so easy to find examples because sales magnets work to increase conversions from a lead to an appointment.

What we've done here is taken what you've been doing naturally for your clients and presented it in a way that the service becomes tangible and easy to understand for a person who doesn't work in the real estate industry daily. In other words, enrolling in a private buyer program that offers access to hidden properties is far more enticing to most people than any individual listing they may be asking you to show them.

In fact, the exclusivity even dampens the enthusiasm they had for the house they're inquiring about because now they're likely wondering what you can show them that they can't see on their own. This is good because the last thing you want to do is go show property to someone who isn't yet a client.

How do they enroll in your private program? Simple. They schedule a time to meet with you in person so you can explain the program in detail and get them enrolled. The only task they need to complete before your meeting is to speak with a lender to get preapproved. When you are going to a listing appointment, you have homework. When a potential buyer is coming to meet you, speaking to a lender is their homework.

The Buyer Consultation: How to Separate Lookers from Buyers

The same process that did the heavy lifting on your listing appointment will do it again for you when you meet with prospective buyers. Your goal at the consultation isn't to get them in your car and sell them a house as fast as you can. Your goal is to lead them through the process so you can determine if this is a client you even want.

Just as sellers do, buyers will travel along a psychological journey during the appointment, and at the end you all will make a mutual decision. When I was in the field, I put even more intention on that mutual decision when meeting with buyers because they were going to take more time and they were going to be in my car. I'm a car guy. What I mean by that is I love to drive my car and take care of it. For as long as I can remember, Friday has been my day to hand wash my car. Some people eat in their cars and wash it only when necessary. I shake the floor mats out daily.

Anyway, my point is, I really never wanted buyers in my car. So if they were there, it meant I really wanted to work with them. Whether you are obsessive (neurotic?) about your automobile or not, you should feel empowered to work only with those buyers you determine you'll enjoy.

THE BUYER'S PSYCHOLOGICAL JOURNEY

Your buyer prospects will move through a psychological journey just as seller prospects do. And like listing appointments, you can't short-cut the journey and expect a favorable outcome. The good news is that staying true to the overall sales process prevents anyone from taking a shortcut.

Remember, no matter what you're selling, the primary sales process you'll use has four parts or stages: take control, find the problem, solve the problem, and close. This is what creates the space necessary for your prospects' journey. The words you use to describe how you're working with the prospect will change with the situation, but the process is the same. So let's look at the journey buyer prospects will take as you guide them.

Stage 1: We're not buying a house today.

That's going to be the mindset of nearly every buyer you meet initially. They're meeting with you because you made an offer, like the direct client program, and they want to start looking. The energy is balanced because, at this moment, you're not sure you want to work with them.

Stage 2: Hey, this agent seems kinda nice.

As you begin working through the appointment, space will be provided for them to relax into your environment, and you'll be able to ask them questions as you begin to investigate their situation and the lifestyle they hope to be living when they close on their new home.

Stage 3: We didn't realize that.

Of course, if you aren't solving any problems for them, why do they need to hire you? There are thousands of agents who will open doors. To set yourself apart, you'll show them how you are the solution to any problem standing in their way that would block the lifestyle they're after.

Stage 4: We sure are glad we met you today.

Now that they have been given space to go over their real estate needs in person with you, their initial skepticism about anything you said on the phone has fallen away. They understand what they will face in the market and how you will help, and now everyone is ready to make a mutual decision. If you want to work with them, you close for the signature.

This process should sound familiar. Take control, find the problem, solve the problem, and close. Remember this is the top-level four-part sales process that never changes. How you execute it depends on who you are meeting so we need to make a few adjustments from our meeting agenda with sellers.

Here is a six-step process to use with prospective buyers. Remember, from the buyer's point of view, this is not a sales process. It's simply the agenda for the appointment and provides comfort in an unusual environment by showing them what to expect.

▶ Step 1: Your Real Estate Lifestyle
▶ Step 2: Buyer Agency
▶ Step 3: The Home Buying Process
▶ Step 4: Live Search
▶ Step 5: Forms
▶ Step 6: Mutual Decision

For the most part, I strongly advocate going through this agenda in an office conference room. I'm well aware that some real estate brokerages don't maintain office space with conference rooms, and even when they do, some clients aren't local. If you don't have access to a conference room at your company, find a meeting space that you can use consistently.

In most cities you can rent coworking spaces, and the rent you pay will be one of your best investments if you actually use the space. Share the expense with another agent if you have to initially, just don't meet at a coffee shop or other public place. It's distracting for people to discuss important issues while surrounded by tables of other people, kids running around, and espresso machines steaming.

It's also disrespectful to the people who may become your clients. Your prospects deserve a professional environment to talk about their home. In the case where you aren't physically in the same city or where there are significant health concerns, you can still use video conferencing to move through the entire process. It's not quite as good as being in the same room, but it can definitely work.

When your potential clients arrive at your meeting place, you are first going to conduct some small talk. Part of taking control is allowing them the space to relax into this foreign environment. When you go to a seller's house, they don't need to relax in their own house. They need space to relax into the appointment because you are in their house.

In this case the buyer needs time to relax because they are in your space. In addition, just like on listing appointments, you don't know what was going on before they got there. They could have had a bad day at work, traffic could have been awful, or they could just be hangry from running around all day. The details of what happened in their day aren't that important. As long as you know there were details, you can't launch into a business discussion until you know they are present in the moment.

Remember how you learned when sellers are present? The same applies here. They will show you physically, and as soon as you notice they're with you, it's time to get to work.

We need to use fear of loss to anchor the importance of the decisions being made. My favorite tool is, once again, the expired list. Most agents think of the expired list as a bunch of disappointed sellers, but there were buyers in the market when those homes were listed, and it's not a stretch to think some of them would have loved to own these houses. It's not the buyers' fault the homes were overpriced and they had to pass over them to others.

Once I realized there was another side to the expired list, I had an idea. I created a visual that was a mix of expired listings, withdrawn listings, and those that came back on the market (BOM). Each of those status categories in your MLS could represent disappointed buyers who didn't get the home they were after and potentially aren't living the life they wanted when they first decided to buy.

Sample dialogue might go like this: "Have you heard of the expired list? It's not a list of dead people. It's people like you who wanted to move and improve their lifestyle. Each of these homes represents a disappointed seller and potentially multiple disappointed buyers. These could have been great homes for people, but along the way, mistakes were made and people had to change or cancel their plans. I can only assume you don't want to be anywhere near a list like this correct? Okay so to get you on the sold list, I've created a simple six-step process. May I share it with you?"

From this point, you show them the six-step meeting agenda overview you've created on your laptop, iPad, or paper and explain how you'll move through each step down to a mutual decision. Once again, when you use the words *mutual decision*, you are implying that you have a choice as well and aren't sitting there begging for their business or dreaming of how you'll spend your commission.

The first step in the consultation process is to ask questions. I'm sure that's no surprise to you at this point. When you're working with buyers, though, it's important to ask a specific kind of open-ended question. I call them "widen the search" questions. Typically agents work to build a wants and needs list so they can go to work finding the perfect house. But as we've discussed, buyers don't know what they want until the moment they walk into it.

Every time they tell you a feature they want in their next property, it narrows the search. Sometimes ridiculously so and you're left with nothing to show them. Here is a list of questions I asked on my own buyer consultations and have coached thousands of others to use with great success:

1. How do you plan to use your home?
2. Do you like to entertain?
3. Do you go out a lot or stay around the house?
4. Where do you like to run around?
5. What is the maximum monthly payment you are comfortable paying?
6. If you needed to pay $ _____ more per month for the perfect house, is that a possibility?
7. Let's daydream a little. What is everything you're hoping to have in your next home?
8. If you had to, what could you live without?
9. What is the maximum amount of cash you have available for the purchase?
10. If you needed $ _____ more down payment, for the perfect house, is that a possibility?
11. If we find the right house today, are you ready to buy it today?

Now let's unpack those questions. Did you notice how they start? The first few questions aren't about bedrooms and bathrooms and floor plans; instead, they're lifestyle-based questions. That's because it's so important to put people before property. Your clients only move because they feel they'll be happier when they are living the lifestyle they've dreamed the new area and home will allow. It's super effective to start the discussion around the lifestyle they are trying to design and then back the conversation into the property itself.

Even if they don't say it, this will cause people to feel like you really understand them. Client loyalty and repeat and referral business should spike as a result, and you'll find yourself operating at consistently higher production levels. The first four questions will give you tremendous insight into the motivations of your prospect.

Question five is an advanced version of a question chronic low producers ask. Low producers always ask, "In what price range are you looking?" Here's the problem: buyers don't know. They know what the lender told them and they know what they've seen online, but unless they're paying cash, people don't buy houses based on the price.

Most of your clients will be taking out a mortgage and that means they will buy based on their comfort level with monthly payment. Modern society is set up so that nearly everything is sold on the monthly payment. Many people don't even buy cars or iPhones these days. They simply budget the monthly payments and trade the item in for a new one each year. So, to be the most helpful to your client, you need to speak in the language that's already in their head: "What is the maximum monthly payment you are comfortable paying?"

The most interesting part about this question is that people can't generally translate sales prices into payments. So their answer will be really helpful to you once you begin the search itself. In any case, whatever they say, it narrows your search dramatically. That's why question number six widens the search: "If you needed X more, is that a possibility?" What you say for X depends on the financial level the buyers happen to be on. If they are first-time home buyers comfortable with $2,000/ month payments, you don't want to ask if paying $2,000 more each month is a possibility. Clearly, it won't be. But if you're working with buyers who are further along in their career and they are comfortable with a $7,000/month payment, for the perfect house, they may magically find $2,000 more. I mean really, how many times have you been certain you'd never pay more than $100 for something and you walk out of the store having paid $397? Happens to me all the time. Especially if I've been shoe shopping.

You'll follow the same pattern for questions seven and eight. The key to question eight is to let them decide what they could live without (such as a fireplace, pool, home office). If you don't try to influence their response, you might be surprised by what they say. I've seen people who were 100 percent certain they must have an in-ground pool tell me if the house was perfect and the neighborhood had a nice pool, they'd consider it.

Questions nine and ten deal with the down payment. Obviously they've had this conversation with the lender and what you're after here is discovery of how much they may have access to, for the perfect house. Often people say they have one amount of money but aren't telling you they have more stashed somewhere to buy furniture. The point is not necessarily to get them to spend all of their furniture money but simply to see if they'd be willing to for the perfect house.

Every time you widen the search, you are doing them a favor. For example, let's say you learn they have an extra $20,000 saved for new furniture that they might consider using if they find a dream home. Okay then, you tell me. Are they going to like the home priced at $299,000 or the one at $320,000 with the better lot?

Now the last question is a gutsy one for sure. "If we find the right house today, are you ready to buy it today?" It's a trial close and super important. That question could cause the buyer to blurt out that they aren't buying a house today. If that happens, just rephrase and soften your trial close by asking if they would at least be willing to make an offer today, should they be lucky enough to find "the one."

That's a little softer version and almost always elicits a "sure, we'd consider it." From time to time, though, you'll get strong pushback to even the suggestion of making an offer. This is a warning sign that you must pay attention to. Lesser agents than you would forge ahead because they fear if they don't, they'll lose the buyer. The problem with that logic is that they don't have a buyer yet. When people tell you they aren't making an offer under any circumstances, they are trying to tell you they aren't ready.

The question then becomes, is it necessary to spend time showing them houses just to stay in a relationship with them? I mean it's your life—oops, I mean time—and if you have that much extra life—oh, I mean time—then by all means, show them homes until the cows come home. To say it plainly, if you don't get a yes at this point, you've got to stop the appointment because they've failed one of the three tests.

Absent any strong objections to making offers, your appointment continues to a quick discussion of agency and then on to a discussion on how you and your team (or your brokerage) will help them through the process. Just like you did for your listing presentation, pick the topics you'd like to present here. Maybe you'll show them a picture of your support team or a diagram of the homebuying process. A visual that leads to a discussion on the inspection process is always a good idea.

Remember, whatever service you choose to show them must be presented as a solution to their problem. The problem is that they want to live the improved lifestyle they have envisioned and it's not possible in their current home. Once you've shown them this part of your presentation, it's time for another trial close: "From what you've seen so far, would anything stop you from teaming up with me to find your next home?"

If you've remained in control and are on track, you usually get a yes. Next, do a live search in the MLS. Every state has an agency disclosure and the beauty about using it here is that it gets your buyers used to signing documents early on in the consultation and eases the path to the big signature on the representation agreement. Even though the buyer can find listings on several sites, there's still a feeling of privilege when logging directly into the MLS. The public can't, and that exclusive access still holds some mystique. Take their widened search criteria and plug it in until you find a list of homes they want to see.

With a list of homes to show them, it's time to cover your buyer representation agreement. This is where you tie in enrollment in the direct client program. How does one enroll? They sign your agreement of course. Remember, no law prevents you from creating your own unique programs, and you could even make it more special by creating a logo for yours.

When you're making this kind of offer, if you aren't a broker, remember to involve your broker so they know what you're putting out to the public. Explain your agreement, hand the buyers the pen, direct them on where to sign, and then get out of their line of sight.

This is the exact moment you have drawn them to the line. You have demonstrated you understand their situation and have stated you are willing to help by offering your services. You've explained how you work and shown them exactly how to become a client. If you plan to show them houses that day, you have the perfect excuse to create space for them to sign because you'll have to make appointments to show these homes they want to see. Step out of the room, make your calls to arrange showings, and come back. Most of the time you'll return to a signed agreement. If not, they've failed test number three.

It might surprise you to learn that I don't talk too much about handling objections when buyers don't want to sign a representation agreement. Does it sound too harsh if I say I just never cared about any objection they might express? Because I truly didn't.

I had a business standard that I was not going into the field with someone until they hired me—in writing. By that point, if they truly didn't feel I was sincerely interested in working as hard as I could for them, we weren't ever going to be a fit, so why try? My only response when a buyer told me they didn't want to sign the agreement was this: "No problem. I'm not trying to make you do anything you don't want to do. The way I do business is to work only for those who hire me in writing. So when you're ready to do that, give me a ring and we can resume."

Sometimes that was it. They left to go waste some other agent's time, and I got my Saturday afternoon back. Other times, the fact that I was willing to cut them loose, straightened them up and they dropped whatever objection they had.

The most important concern here is to do what you need to do to develop the mindset that you deserve commitment. Look, I understand that a good attorney could probably get any buyer out of almost any buyer rep agreement. Whether it's an iron-clad agreement or not isn't the point. If a buyer isn't willing to give you the commitment you deserve for all of the time and energy I know you'll pour into them, you're better off letting them go and finding someone who will appreciate you. In any case, it'll free up time to build your listing inventory.

One of the challenges in writing this chapter about sales methodologies was to resist the temptation to tell you everything I've learned over the years about sales. In a perfect world, I'd be able to spend countless hours with you in private coaching. We'd use your experiences in the field as triggers to get all of that knowledge downloaded into your brain.

Then I realized, when it comes to the specific ways you work with buyers and sellers, if you commit to revisiting this section often, over time you'll learn most of what I'd have passed on to you in coaching. Working with a private coach is no doubt a faster way to learn, but it's not the only way. However you go about it, I can promise you this: investing time in mastering your sales methodologies will always pay off.

The two business macros I've discussed so far—mindset and sales methodologies—have teed us up for the third and this final macro, which can be like pouring gasoline on the fire. When in alignment with the other two, the third macro, marketing, can add the fuel you need to build your career as big as you can dream.

6

▼

Marketing Tactics:
A Timeless Framework
for Unlimited Growth

Real estate agents everywhere are suffering from an addiction to get-rich-quick marketing tactics. Many agents have sold themselves on the idea that if they use a magic combination of marketing tactics and post enough on social media, they don't need to learn how to sell.

This way of thinking crept in slowly over time as technology companies have consistently played into your fear of being seen as a salesperson, working hard to convince you that you need them. And today, we've reached the point where, when your business macros are out of balance, it's as easily identifiable as a car with steering that's out of alignment.

Specifically, when an agent is relying too heavily on marketing, you can see them jump from one tactic to another, or as I described earlier, they've fallen into the try-this trap. Every tactic that comes along can seem so promising and exciting, especially if you watch the success stories on the sales pages. But have you ever placed an ad online and watched how fast your budget is used up?

If sales were as easy as placing an ad and watching leads rain down from the internet gods, we wouldn't have much to discuss here. Everyone has at one time spent money on an ad online and wondered what happened except for a few measly clicks.

The idea that we could post content online and run a few targeted ads, then have the perfect business, makes about as much sense as eating a dozen Krispy Kreme donuts all day and expecting to have a perfect body for the beach. To be sure, at the beginning of my career, I couldn't send a bunch of post-cards at random and expect a ton of leads either. So in that way, nothing has changed. But now that our world is so driven by technology, we seem to think we can take a class on Instagram and learn how to get a million followers or post stories that quickly translate to business.

That's fascinating to me because I never remember going to a class on how to send postcards to get leads. And isn't a postcard the analog version of an Instagram post? Obviously adding technology to marketing has made it highly addictive.

Put simply, relying too heavily on marketing tactics in relation to your other business macros will make your business bloated and your balance sheet very unhealthy. I'm not a marketing expert and you don't need to be either. Just like you don't need to be a nutritionist to understand how to consume carbohydrates in a way that benefits your health, you don't need a marketing degree to keep your tactics in balance in your business. But you do need to be mindful of the temptations out there. The entire reason the try-this trap exists is because people naturally seek the easy way out. Jumping from one tactic to another until your money runs out is no different than jumping from one diet to the next. You won't generate a steady stream of leads and you won't lose weight. This is why you won't find this section full of clever marketing tactics. Thriving businesses aren't built on tactics, they're built on principles. Instead, we're going to look at a framework that will help you build a marketing strategy around principles that don't throw you out of balance.

I'm going to show you a way to think about marketing that allows for plenty of choice and creativity so that as technology evolves, you can make choices that are right for you and not risk becoming influenced by the agendas of everyone wanting your money.

Front-End versus Back-End Marketing

Front-end marketing brings you new leads, and back-end marketing helps you stay connected to, and in relationship with, your database.

For most of our industry's history, people lumped the two together. The tactics we employed to find new leads were basically the same tactics we used to follow up with our leads and past clients. We made follow-up calls and sent listing-based marketing. We used just-listed and sold cards, magazine and newspaper ads, and market update newsletters. Some people incorporated lifestyle messages such as basic tax tips in April or football schedules in the fall.

When marketing moved online, at first it was just more of the same tactics but in a digital format. In any case, as creative as it's gotten, nearly all marketing in real estate is focused on listings. It's so focused on listings that when agents don't have a listing, marketing suffers. That's because other than football schedules, a list of events around town, and time change reminders, agents aren't given much guidance on how to use their voice in marketing.

Coming Out from behind the Listing

As you've learned, sales magnets are ideas that have been given a name, are reduced to a visual, and used to persuade people. So far I've discussed using them to persuade prospects to schedule an appointment, and we've looked at how they persuade people to overcome their fear of signing agreements.

Now we need to discuss them in terms of your front-end marketing because they are key to coming out from behind the listing. In this context, your sales magnet is some kind of advertisement that makes an offer to connect with people. In real estate, listings were the original sales magnets, and promoting them has always been more about generating leads than selling the house. If you want leads in any business, you have to make offers to connect with new people. Listings should always be a part of your front-end marketing strategy, and you can jump ahead of your competition if you're willing to push a little further.

List building is a term that comes from internet marketing and refers to activities that get people to subscribe to your email list for the purposes of developing a relationship with and eventually making a sale to them. If you've ever scrolled through social media and stopped on an ad to give them your email address in exchange for a free report, you've been added to someone's list.

Most people who work in internet marketing are selling products and services with far shorter sales cycles than residential real estate, but the concept is the same one top producing agents have been using since the beginning of our industry. I've used information about listings instead of free reports and different terminology like "our database" instead of "our email list," but the differences don't go much deeper than that.

The problem for most agents is that the listing is the primary trigger to do any kind of marketing other than vanity ads with no offer or call to action. So unless there is an active listing to promote, marketing is likely inconsistent. More than ever before, you have a chance to expand beyond the listing, and the best way is to come out from behind it.

When I was a young man and realized the feelings I was having during puberty meant that I was gay, I panicked about how I was going to come out of the closet. When I did so, I felt totally exposed and vulnerable but also liberated and free. That's not a dissimilar set of feelings experienced by agents who begin to use their voice and express their point of view in the marketplace. To "come out" from behind the listings means you're going to feel a bit exposed, but it's the only way you'll feel the full freedom your business can offer.

Information has exploded in every industry, and it's only getting more intense, which means people are drowning in information and crave context and opinion. Real estate marketing has traditionally offered information only and no context. The consumer is dying for you to come out. They need you to be yourself, express your opinions, and help them make sense of all this information flooding them.

Think of it this way: if I saw a strange spot on my skin and searched the image online, I definitely want to know my doctor's opinion of all this information I just found. I know she can't predict any outcome with certainty, but still, I want to hear her professional opinion. And buyers and sellers want yours. The more you can show up in this way, the more you'll position yourself as the expert—and remember, it's the experts that people refer and rehire. All you need is your creativity and a touch of bravery to use your voice.

When we share our opinions, we are naturally positioned as the expert in the minds of people in our market. Simply publishing a blog post helps make you an expert. Whenever I ask agents for their opinion on the market, they always have one, and it's a shame that it's often not shared. Some agents are initially worried about being wrong or that sharing an opinion opens them up to criticism. But to show up as an expert, you have to think deeper into the content you are using.

When you send market data, ask what it means to you. When news hits about real estate, how do you look at its potential impact for the people you serve? When you answer those questions, your next task is to decide how you want to offer your answers to the public. It can be as simple as an infographic or a short pdf in the form of a free report.

I'm not talking about the monthly market statistics infographics your board of Realtors® publishes. You can certainly use those in your marketing, but the idea is to make a unique offer to connect from your point of view and in your voice that can be found nowhere else. This is the kind of offer that will draw the people you most enjoy serving to you like a magnet.

Let's pull this together with an example. Imagine you love working in a part of town that's in high demand and want to connect with more leads for that area, but you don't have a listing yet (or you do and you're trying to come out from behind it). Remember, people buy houses because of the lifestyle they think they'll have when they are living in them. Think of an area in your town that is highly walkable and is known for its fantastic restaurants.

While your competition advertises themselves and their listings, you can take a different approach. You could create a Happy Hour Guide where people can take themselves on a self-guided tour of spots you handpick for them based on your area expertise, complete with your recommendation on the best dishes at each restaurant, the best time and day to go, a note about who has the best specials, and which places to avoid. You could deliver the guide via a free infographic or flyer that lays out your recommendations.

You could go even further by including a link to a custom Google map where you've marked the spots you recommend with your personal tips included. Once you've created your offer (the sales magnet), it's time to get it ready for delivery to your prospects, and that is most commonly done with a landing page. Think of a landing page as a one-page website designed for a singular purpose: to present your sales magnet and ask for a name and email address.

In this case, you would make your offer to receive a free Happy Hour Self-Guided Tour. All they have to do is give you their email address and, bingo, you now have a new lead to nurture. Odds are, your brokerage already has software to help you create landing pages, and, if not, a simple internet search will give you tons of options.

To live a Top Producer Life, you are going to have to learn how to use your voice and experiment with the offers you put into the marketplace. Coming out from behind the listing means you are no longer going to hide your opinions from your prospects and clients, and it also means you'll no longer be restricted in marketing to listings.

At this point, you no doubt understand that translating your ideas and opinions into effective sales magnets will take practice. In the meantime, I encourage you to use the Happy Hour Self-Guided Tour, or any derivative it inspires you to create such as tours of the best area food trucks or locally owned shops. Until you develop the ability to develop information for your sales magnet instinctively, ask yourself these three questions:

1. What problem(s) would this sales magnet (piece of marketing) solve?
2. If I were a buyer or seller, would this information help me?
3. Have I included a clear call to action?

Consider how the Happy Hour Self-Guided Tour solves problems. Someone who really wants to live in an area is probably running around in it long before they buy a house there. As they explore, they will no doubt seek the best places to eat. This sales magnet solves the problem of information overload and gives them back their time to visit more places instead of using it for research.

Let's say a buyer prospect has a choice: one agent is offering to set them up on a search for new homes that hit the market and the other sends them on a tour of the area to have good drinks and eat good food. Umm, is this really a choice? I mean, these days they can set themselves up on a home search through several different websites if that's what they really want.

Once you have a sales magnet created, you can use a combination of paid and free marketing to get the offer out there and seen by people. No one ever knows which offer will perform the best, and any given idea may totally bomb. But it might not and you'll only know if you try. The more you make offers like this, the better you'll get at using your voice to generate new leads with your front-end marketing.

When you're ready and have the budget, you can leverage the creation of your sales magnets to others, but because the ideas are coming from you, your prospects will still be hearing your voice.

BACK-END MARKETING

Back-end marketing is made up of all the tactics you use to stay connected to people in your database when they aren't actively looking to buy or sell a home. The goal of back-end marketing isn't to stay connected just for the sake of it; you want to stay connected in order to generate referrals and repeat business. Back-end marketing is how you access the full lifetime value of a client.

The main takeaway here is that your biggest opportunity in marketing is on the back end. I remember my broker going through the office on what she called the postcard cleanup. She'd do this every so often because some of the agents in my office had a bad habit of buying postcard marketing programs and then not sending the stuff out. Remember these were pre-internet days, and we lacked the automation that exists today.

Not only did boxes of unsent postcards look trashy under our desks, but they weren't doing anyone any good sitting there. I remember arriving at the office early one day before the sales meeting watching her carry the boxes to the front of the meeting room and stacking them with agents' names on them. We played some sort of game that morning, and those who won were given postage allowances to make us get them out of the office and into the mail.

From the broker's point of view, every postcard sitting in a box was a missed opportunity for a sale. What I didn't learn until later is that, worse than missed sales, inconsistency registers as untrustworthiness in the subconscious mind and that's exactly where you don't want it to register. People in your database won't be able to say why, but they won't feel compelled to refer you when the opportunity arises if some part of their brain is telling them you can't be trusted.

I touched on this when we talked about the secrets to generating referrals. If you're inconsistent with your front-end marketing efforts, it's not as damaging because you're working to make an initial contact with someone. But once contact is made and they are in your database, it's a different story.

About a year ago I spoke to an agent who told me he needed to get back to his regular mailings. I'm on his mailing list and what he sent shortly after looked like he was trying to catch up. Two months of predesigned flyers were stuffed into one envelope with a cover letter, and even though I like the guy a lot and know he's a great agent, I picked up on a feeling that he can't keep his business together.

When salespeople get in the habit of focusing primarily on the next deal, back-end marketing becomes an afterthought. The problem is compounded by the fact that the lead cycle is so long in real estate, once someone buys a house, they don't need you for a while. And that's too bad because it ignores the lifetime value of a client. Part of that value is the new people they can connect you to in between their own moves.

If you stay consistent with your back-end marketing and don't forget to include consistent follow-up calls, your effort should pay off well. On one level, showing up consistently with nearly anything will get you fairly far. I remember the first time I wanted to send a newsletter to my database. My just-listed and sold postcards were on autopilot, and I was ready to step it up a bit. There was far less automation then and color printing was still noticeably more expensive than black and white. But my ego was on the line with this newsletter because I spent a ton of time designing it.

I obsessed for about a month getting it just right before I printed it in color on high-quality paper. The printing was done on my office's new color printer so I was charged a little less than if I went to a commercial operation. When I was done, an office buddy named Andy came up behind me and printed off his newsletters in black and white, on regular copy machine paper. You know, the kind that doesn't hold up too well to post office sorting machines.

Andy was a top producer, not just in my company but in the whole city, and when I asked why he would send out such low-quality newsletters with his name on it, he laughed and responded, "Jasen, they don't read them. I just need them to see my name. While everyone else wastes time on beautiful creations like you have in your hand, my team goes out on appointments."

There was no arguing with the numbers. Andy was way ahead of me at the time and, thankfully, his lesson sank in. The lesson is a humbling one that every top producer must learn; people will give the marketing pieces you worked so hard on mere seconds before they hit delete or pitch them in the recycle bin. If they see your name and a blurb about real estate, even for a split second, you can count it as a success. Consistency is about the only thing you can control that will have any meaningful impact.

The Key to More Repeat Clients

Whether you have been conscious of it or not, all back-end marketing activities serve as sales magnets for repeat and referral business. The difference now is that you can be deliberate about your efforts to use them that way instead of leaving your marketing to chance. Although as I mentioned before, sending out old school style newsletters and generic prewritten market updates will work to a degree, I'm not so confident that I'll be able to say that for too much longer. For the moment, if all you can do is buy a subscription to a service that will produce a back-end marketing piece for you, then by all means do it. It will certainly be better than nothing as long as you remain consistent.

At this point, I trust I've sold you on how harmful it is to skip a month. So just set a standard for yourself that you don't skip months. People grow in stages in real estate, and generic, prewritten, done-for-you marketing can be an effective place-holder if you are working hard to build momentum in your career and get your commission income steady.

Eventually, you'll want to infuse your back-end marketing with your unique voice just like one would for front-end marketing. In this case I think it's even more important because presumably you have a relationship with these folks already. So wouldn't you want to do better than just flood them with even more information?

Time and attention is the most valuable commodity someone can give you and deserves to be respected. Every time I get a generic newsletter from my insurance agent, I'm reminded of what I'd never want you to do. Insurance companies are set up by design to guard against loss. It's a very scarcity-based industry and that's why you may never see your insurance agent send you a marketing piece with their opinions. That would never make it past their legal department so they have no choice but to send out boring crap we all just throw away or delete.

You don't have to send your marketing past legal for clearance, so the way to infuse your voice into your back-end marketing is to ask the following:

- ▶ What can I say that has the potential to add real value and stimulate thought?
- ▶ Would I want to get this?
- ▶ Is there a clear call to action?

In a way, echo chambers on the internet have made it incredibly difficult for people to feel safe using their voice. When you're never exposed to anyone who holds an opposing point of view, it's easy to think of disagreement as bad. But agreement from everyone isn't necessary for you to use your voice in your back-end marketing. In fact, total agreement with your opinions is counterproductive for the people you wish to serve. It's the problem insurance companies have.

If your marketing material is purposely as bland as possible, written with a total lack of opinions so there's literally no possibility of disagreement, then the end result is junk mail and a wasted opportunity to help people grow. You see, when I know what you think about a topic, it's easier for me to get clear on what I think, especially if I don't totally agree with you. Rather than showing up as junk, your opinions stimulate thought, and if you're really lucky, conversation, which keeps your relationships engaged and fresh. It's possible to be provocative, interesting, kind, and professional at the same time.

To drive that point home, sometimes in coaching I'll discuss the difference between an argument and a fight. These days, many people conflate the two and, as a result, fear their own voice.

When you fight with someone, your goal is to win. But when you argue, your goal is to win them over. That's a distinct difference and to me it means arguing is just sales. When we argue, the goal is to persuade someone to agree with our way of thinking, to sell them on seeing the situation our way. This entire book is an argument meant to persuade you to look at sales the way I do and sell you on adopting the material in your own practice. I'm not so confused as to think you would agree with every single word I've written.

Pop culture thrives on people wearing their emotions on their sleeves, and the mere thought of someone "coming for you" puts people in attack mode. That might be funny online but, unfortunately, I've had a front row seat to its destructive effect in business. Everyone has become afraid to use their voice because we've forgotten how to argue with (sell, persuade) each other in a healthy way.

I've found there is just no way agents will expand beyond boring template-driven back-end marketing until they've done the internal work necessary to connect with their own voice and drum up the courage to use it. Part of this work entails dropping the concern over what others think of us. Social media have caused huge numbers of people to fall victim to imposter syndrome and dim their own light as they compare themselves to everyone else's highlight reel.

Ultimately, we all have private thoughts, and there is immense freedom in simply acknowledging that fact and allowing others to think what they want to think. They are going to do it anyway and so are you. This is why I've always found it silly when people worry about their reputation. You can't control your reputation any more than you can control the thoughts of other people. You can only control your own thoughts and actions. So what's left is to perform in the marketplace with integrity, to do the right thing, serve people as best you can, and treat people with kindness.

If you do that and someone wants to attempt to trash your reputation, let them. They can't do you any real harm. As they speak negatively about you, they are simply exposing themselves as bitter and negative and everyone will see it. Stay above all of that and focus on you. The truth is, the biggest challenge isn't dealing with people trying to trash your reputation with negative comments, it's dealing with the way we trash our own thinking with an overabundance of concern of what others are thinking.

I can tell you this for sure: nearly every day I can point to evidence that shows society rewards those who are brave enough to express themselves. The fact that so few people do, combined with the fact that consumers crave it, leaves you with a massive opportunity.

So let's say you've been persuaded by my argument. What now? Now go back to those focusing questions and experiment. What is going on in the world or in your market that you feel inspired to discuss? What you choose can be explicitly related to real estate or it could be about current events within your market or it can even be about you personally.

Some of the best back-end marketing I've seen pulls together a mix of opinions on news and current events in the area, market statistics with an interpretation of their meaning for people, a little about the agent living their life, some testimonials from recent clients, and promotion of properties listed. It takes more work to create a marketing piece like that, but the other option is to show up as boring and unremarkable.

Your Marketing Framework: Stay Creative and Avoid Stress from Technology

As you can tell by now, I'm not concerned about any particular marketing tactic you use and never intended to write about tactics because as soon as I published the book, they have changed. Tactics come and go just like new kinds of carb-filled snacks come and go. When I was a kid we'd eat Cracker Jacks, Moon Pies, Twinkies, and Ding Dongs, but I haven't seen any advertising for these in years. Honestly I have no idea what kids eat these days, but whatever it is, it's just more sugar, flour, and vegetable oil presented with a new tactic. Get it?

So as clever marketers come up with ever more creative ways for us to reach people, you are free to pick and choose what resonates with you. As long as you plug those tactics into your framework, you'll avoid the try-this trap. Remember, this is your practice and you should feel free to take the framework and make it your own. Add to it, subtract from it, whatever you're inspired to do. Just make sure that whatever you build for yourself, you commit to and execute consistently. Start as small as you need because you can always add more as your practice grows.

Start with the front end of your marketing.

CONNECT TO NEW PEOPLE

The first items to build out are your offers to connect to new people. This includes all of the marketing you do for your listings. The tactics that you use to market your listings are always going to be effective offers to connect with new leads, and they will naturally be the ones your sellers are most interested in seeing.

The easiest way to implement your listing-based advertising is to take your chosen tactics and design a ninety-day plan that repeats itself. In strong sellers' markets, you won't get anywhere near items at the end of that third month. In strong buyers' markets, you may work through that plan twice before the listing goes under contract. A repeating ninety-day plan will keep you disciplined and give you confidence to communicate with your clients in any market conditions.

This means you'll need to decide where and how you'll market your listing inventory. Will you go digital only? Digital and print media? How specifically will you use social media? Taking the time to write out what you'll do is important because if you don't, you'll spend money randomly and you'll constantly be in a state of low-grade stress about what you're doing to sell your listings. Top producers don't ever worry about that because they build out their marketing plans and then put it on autopilot.

OFFER TO BUILD RELATIONSHIPS

When someone inquires about your listing or your custom sales magnet, they have given you permission to market to them, and it's important not to waste the opportunity. To do that, you'll need to design a relationship building sequence of five to seven messages delivered over the course of ten to fourteen days. The goal of these messages is to get into relationship with the person (build rapport) and determine if they are planning a move in either the near or distant future.

If you determine the move is not far off, the third piece to design is a follow-up plan that causes you to stay close to the lead. Your messages should be weekly if not more frequent and built out, remembering the conversion chain. If you discover your new lead has a move occurring sometime in the distant future, once you've sent them the sequence that builds up the relationship, you'll move them to your back-end marketing.

BACK-END MARKETING

Back-end marketing has five pieces to build out. If someone is receiving your back-end marketing, it means they are in your book of business, and hopefully at this point, you naturally care about sending messages that in some way improve their life or brighten their day. When you are choosing your tactics for this part of the framework, remember to ask yourself: Would I want to get this? Could this in any way show up as a pleasant surprise?

Piece 1: Flagship Content: Your flagship content is what your book of business will become most familiar with. It could be a monthly newsletter, your weekly video post, or even a podcast. Currently, my flagship content is a weekly video message sent to my database each Sunday designed to help people set the tone for a successful week.

Having a strategy for flagship content doesn't mean you can't do other messaging, but it does mean one item will be most important. You're only ever going to get so much attention from your audience, so make your flagship content the place where you really shine. For example, I love writing blog posts and I love speaking. That's why I chose to send vlog-style videos as my flagship content each Sunday to my database. It doesn't mean I can't release a podcast and it doesn't mean I can't post long form, written blog posts. It's just that those items won't be my flagship content; other tactics are designed to accent it.

Piece 2: Phone + Text + DM + Personal Notes: When people think of marketing, they often make the mistake of limiting their thinking to a piece of paid advertising that is broadcast to a wide audience. But marketing can be intimate and individualized too.

To maintain relevance and a strong connection with your database, personal attention will put you miles ahead of any competitor that comes along. Calling someone just to say hello and sending personal notes and text messages and direct messages on social media all fall into the marketing category.

To build out this piece, you'll want a plan that keeps you engaged in these activities throughout the year. A good rule of thumb is to connect with each person once a quarter individually. You won't always reach everyone, but it's the attempt that counts. The good news is that nearly all of the modern CRM systems have templated plans for this type of communication just waiting for your customizations.

Piece 3: In Person: My first client party wasn't just mine; at the time I couldn't afford it by myself. So I shared the expense with a few other agents, and we threw a real estate party together. Later on I was at a real estate conference and heard an agent on a panel say she rented out a movie theater and did a movie night for her clients. I thought that was brilliant and went about building a similar event to serve as my in-person marketing.

Once a year, instead of throwing a traditional client party, I hosted a movie night during the summer, and it was one of the biggest lead generators of the year. If large-scale events aren't your style, there are other ways to get face time with your database. Catching up over coffee, lunch, or dinner works and you could even stop by their home and say hello for a few minutes with a small gift. Seeing people in person is never as easy or frequent as email marketing, but it's super high impact and worth thinking about how you'll do it from the start.

Piece 4: Special Treatment for A and A+: Remember that marketing on the back end is multipurposed. It should help you generate referrals and repeat business and should help you stay in relationship with people. As I discussed before, not all relationships are equal in business. Those that support you with their own business and with their referrals deserve special attention.

For this piece, you'll need to build out a plan for your most important supporters, your As and A+s. There are infinite ways you could do this. You could give them advance notice of a client party or early heads-up on a great investment property you're about to list. The goal is to make these people feel really special.

Here's an example: My As and A+s received early invitations to my yearly client party, which for many years was a movie night. I'd always rent the biggest theater in the movie house so I had roughly 350 tickets to give out, and these folks got a few days to reserve as many tickets as they wanted.

One year, a past client who always advocated for me called to see if he could bring a few people from his department at work, and he reserved three tickets. That particular summer, the movie was one of the Marvel superhero releases, and his department was made up of programmers in their midtwenties at IBM. When the first three people talked about coming to the movie, they all wanted to come. My client called back to see if there was any way a few more could come.

Because he was an A+ I asked how many people were in his department. His answer was twenty-five so I gave him twenty-five tickets. Over the next eighteen months, all but four of them became clients.

Piece 5: Referral Encouragement: The last piece is your referral encouragement marketing. Many years ago I knew an agent who received a good number of referrals and always made a big deal of sending a gift to the person who sent the referral after the deal closed. The problem with this is that the people who send you referrals can't control if the deal closes or not. Because of that, it's always better to reward the behavior you want.

To reward people who sent me referrals, I approached a local car wash and got permission to print custom and numbered gift certificates with my branding on them. We arranged for their accounting department to send me the redeemed certificates with a bill once each month. The arrangement worked well, and I sent those certificates out the same day any referral came in.

Marketing can be fun and uncomplicated when kept in balance. If you remember to use your voice creatively and practice building sales magnets, you'll have the raw material you need to create advertising for your front-end marketing. That's in addition to your standard ninety-day marketing plan for listings that also serves as front-end marketing. Then, when you've decided what you'll do for each of the five pieces of your back-end marketing, you'll have a built-out framework that will serve you for years.

As technology changes, you can add or subtract as needed. Beyond that, a few concepts, discussed next, closely related to marketing will help you deliver messages in the right way and in the right tone.

HOMELAND VERSUS EMBASSY

Some aspects of marketing you have complete control over, and with others you have literally zero control. For example, you control your own database and the information it contains. You also control your own URL and any print media you create yourself. But you have zero control over Google, all social media, and even print publications in which you advertise. Those are platforms owned by other companies and those companies determine the rules. So it would be foolish to put too much energy into building a massive following on social media without also spending at least as much energy building your own database.

Have you ever heard of someone getting locked out of Facebook for violating the rules? It's happened to me a couple of times, and I have no clue what rule I broke. It's not like Facebook publishes a list for us to reference. Worse than that, I've known people who had their business pages taken from them and deleted with no warning. You cannot give that amount of control over your business to other people.

To keep you from making that mistake, think of what you own and control (your own website and database) as your Homeland. Every other platform is one of your Embassies. The United States has embassies all over the world, but if shit goes down in another country, we could lose our embassy overnight. That's not going to happen in our Homeland. So the main function of a US Embassy is to promote the interests of our country abroad and direct activity back into our Homeland. The same is true for your business.

Online advertising and all social media should function as your Embassies. Their main function is to promote the interest of your Homeland and direct people back to it. Functionally, when you run an ad on Facebook with any offer to connect, that should direct people back to a landing page on your own website (your Homeland) to get it or, at the very least, capture their contact information so you can begin sending them messages from your Homeland; in this case that could be email marketing.

Or if you post a success story with clients on Instagram, it should reference your own website as often as possible. This way, when the rules change without notice, you won't lose your connection to your own business. For these reasons, your flagship content should always live on a platform you own. From there, it can be shared with your Embassies like your Facebook business page or YouTube channel.

YOU DON'T HAVE TO BE A GURU

When some people become an agent, they think it means they all of a sudden must act like some sort of guru or motivational speaker. Now, if you want to be seen as a guru, I certainly won't discourage you, but realize that has nothing to do with being an effective agent. For most people, you are just their agent and that's it. People aren't looking to real estate agents for life coaching and they aren't counting on you to serve as their source of inspiration.

Even though we real estate agents joke about having to be marriage counselors during a transaction, clients aren't really looking for that either. What they want is a professional who will focus on them, keep their own ego out of the picture, and just help them realize the lifestyle they envision living in the new home. Agents living the Top Producer Life get this. Agents have an unshakable faith that when they help clients access the lifestyle they want, they too gain access to the lifestyle they want.

Part of growing as a professional is realizing that not everyone you work for is going to be your best friend. Not everyone is going to come to your client party or like your page/profile on social media. I remember my broker giving it to me straight when I was in my midtwenties.

She said: "Young man, your clients don't care about the Jasen show. They aren't going to be your best friend and most won't even be friends. You are there to serve them and that's it. Just because they don't come to your client party doesn't mean they don't appreciate your work. It also doesn't mean they won't refer you and rehire you again. But Jasen, you're just their agent."

That was hard to hear but also made a lot of sense once someone cared enough to tell me. After all, I have no interest in being friends with every service professional in my life, so why should I expect others to want to be besties with me? Now I'm not a total asshole and some of my clients have become friends, really good friends even who have stayed at my house, but for most, I was the professional and they were the client, end of story. In fact, some people don't want to do business with friends, so if you try to make everyone yours, you're likely missing out on business.

But social media have not only given a new definition to the word *friends*, these platforms have given everyone a voice. We're all given this illusion of connection and friendship blurring the lines between client and professional that at one time were pretty darn clear. Given that I just worked to persuade you to use your voice, I want to be clear I'm not doing an about-face. Frankly my intent here is to keep you from getting too full of yourself, just like my broker did for me. When it comes to marketing, we have to remember to focus on the client, not on our own ego, and in terms of social media, we each have to decide how we are going to use our platforms.

When I first started with Facebook and Twitter, I viewed social media almost exclusively through the lens of my business. I was a traveling speaker and coach at that point and used it as a way to stay connected to my students who were all over the country. When Instagram came along, I chose to use that for personal creativity. These days, Facebook is still strictly for business and Instagram is a mix of personal and professional so those who are interested have a way to get to know me better.

However you choose to use your platforms, remember that authenticity is incredibly important. When speaking and writing, don't present yourself as anything other than what you are because you won't be able to keep up an act forever. Eventually, someone will see the real you anyway, and if there's any discrepancy, trust will be broken immediately. This is why when I see agents working hard to craft an image online that is engineered, I do my best to help them see the dangers of that approach.

The most obvious example is when new agents begin posting as if they are somehow instantly successful. Our industry does a poor job of developing salespeople to begin with, and it's made worse when we give all the attention to the super successful agents. It's my opinion that this triggers new agents to feel compelled to present themselves as successful from day one when everyone, including the public, knows better.

I don't notice other service-based professions doing this as much. I've never seen a personal trainer act as if they've got it together right out of the gate. On the contrary, they hustle and people respect them for it. When I'm working with new agents, one of my most common messages is to be proud you are new. You're only new once and there is unique energy that comes along with it that can be used to your advantage.

People love to help others go for their dreams. People love helping others who demonstrate hustle because, in a way, it inspires us all to think bigger. But all of that is lost when you act like you're a success before you've paid your dues. If you broadcast the message you don't need people right off the bat, guess what? They won't help you, even though, on some level, they know you need it. It's the wrong way to use your voice and now you're off the hook. Be transparent, be yourself, and be proud of it!

LEARN, THEN LEVERAGE

Online advertising is a massive profession in and of itself, and the situation has gotten far more complicated. However, there are great benefits to this as well. We've never been able to reach just the right people so quickly before. When you get into real estate, you quickly learn there is so much more to learn than you ever dreamed when you were getting your license, and because of that, it's easy for someone with a little bit of money to pay someone to do online marketing for you.

This is a huge mistake I see so many people make. Using leverage in business is good, but you aren't leveraging anything if you don't know what's going on in the first place. That's a sure way to get taken advantage of and waste tons of money. Such practices have been going on since before social media.

I remember heavy hitters in my real estate office paying $50,000 to $60,000 for websites that took forever, never seemed to be finished, and didn't amount to much more than a very expensive online brochure that not many people saw. So whether it's web design or social media ad campaigns, if you intend to be a responsible business owner and truly employ leverage in your practice, you're going to have to gain a base level of knowledge so you understand what needs to be done and can recognize it when you see it being done.

You'll need to create some of your own sales magnets, build some landing pages, and run some ads online until you've had some success. It means you may need to take online courses yourself while you're experimenting and give yourself the benefit of time to learn. The good news here is that the large players like Facebook and Google have their own courses built that you can take for free.

With enough determination, you'll eventually reach a point where you realize you've got the basics down. Then, as your budget allows, you can seek the services that will execute the basics for you on a higher level. Only this way, you'll know when you're getting what you paid for.

The Four Offers

Throughout various parts of this book I've used the word *offers* in a context separate from offers on real estate. In business, there are four basic offers that all top producers learn to develop. Although it's possible to let your practice get complicated, it's not really necessary. Almost always, staying focused on a few simple and basic concepts makes all the difference. So as you work on building up and refining your individual practice, keep an eye on these four types of offers.

1. **Offer to connect**. Whether it's paid advertising, direct prospecting, or posting on social media, the content you create in these areas is an offer to connect. Everything you can think of that is lead generating in nature is your way of persuading someone to connect with you.

2. **Offer to build a relationship**. Once a person connects with you, it's your job to nurture that connection so that a business relationship develops. All of your follow-up efforts and everything you do to stay connected with your database is an offer to build relationships.

3. **Offer to do business**. The ultimate goal of the first two offers is to get to a point where the people you're connected to schedule appointments with you. It's on those appointments, using what you learned about your methodology business macro, where you make an offer to do business with people. Anytime you ask for a signature on a listing or buyer representation agreement, you've made an offer to do business.

4. **Offer to refer and rehire**. Longer term, all of the methods you use to stay connected to people between moves is an offer to serve when a referral needs to be made and when past clients need to move again.

Part III

Living Your Top Producer Life

7

Your Transformation

When one of my mentors conferred upon me the rank of master salesperson, I remember a temporary feeling of completion. Sort of like I'd made it after all the years of work. Growth and transformation only stop when we die. Our choice is to learn to use the energy of transformation to our advantage or to fight it.

By energy of transformation I mean life itself. Those you would consider a master have likely chosen to use the energy of life productively. They'll also tell you that mastery is really an elusive concept because the more you master a skill, the more you discover to learn. That's probably why these days I really like the word *transformation* more than *mastery*. For most people, to master something implies the work is done, but true masters know that's never the case.

You are going to go on your own transformational journey that will come in three stages: momentum building, skill building, and then living from mastery. When you understand what happens at each stage along the path, you can design your journey for yourself.

Stage One: Momentum Building

Living as a top producer starts with momentum building, and it's the most difficult part of the path to the career you've envisioned. As a plane barrels down the runway toward takeoff, it must burn a ton of fuel to hit a specific ground speed before tilting the nose up, and it must do that against the wind. Once airborne a lot more fuel must be burned to get to cruising altitude where cruising can finally settle down a bit.

This is exactly what the beginning of your career will feel like. Momentum building is a bit of a hustle and frankly a bit of a hot mess. The key is to start where you are and realize that wherever that is, someone can take your circumstances and succeed with them, so why not you? The most important business macro at this stage of growth is mindset because you'll have to use your thoughts to find your way to a state of belief in your own success before you see physical evidence of it.

I started with no network to speak of and acne all over my face. Others have moved to a new city where they knew no one and started their path during a recession. If we can do it, so can you. When building momentum, it's important to find a primary mentor and put yourself on an information diet. Karate and Aikido are both martial arts, but you wouldn't study them at the same time. The same is true for your business development. You can't build much momentum when you have more than one mentor guiding you in different ways. It's not that one mentor is better (or more right) than the other. It's that this stage is hard enough without having to sort through different opinions.

Find a mentor with whom you resonate and stick with him or her. Ideally, you want a mentor who understands that momentum building is about massive action. It's about activity level, not skill level. For example, when you learn to play tennis, after a few basic lessons, the objective is to hit as many tennis balls as possible. It's more important to play a ton than it is to obsess over your footwork or the intricacies of your serve. A good coach would know when to step in and focus on specific skills.

In real estate, the easiest way to get your activity up and build momentum is to spend the majority of your time in lead generation mode. At this level you have to go way beyond an hour and well past noon working to generate leads. When I'm coaching people, the trigger to move forward is when the agent starts to consistently schedule three appointments per week. With that level of activity, it's possible to start doing meaningful skill building. Much less than that and it's like trying to get good at tennis by playing only occasionally. It just won't happen.

I remember when I was first challenged to go on three appointments a week. I did the math and realized that would be twelve per month. At that point I hadn't been on twelve appointments in eighteen months, and the goal seemed impossible. But of course everything's impossible until someone does it. No one thought it was possible to run a mile in under four minutes until Roger Bannister did in 1954. Now more than 1,400 people have claimed to have done it.

As impossible as that many appointments seemed to me, I had to admit that there were people around me who consistently were going on three appointments in a week. If there was one person, there could be two, and I could be number two. It took a while and some long days on the phone, maybe even some tears on the way home, but I made it happen. When you're burning that much fuel, not only do you get the chance to start some real skill building, but each transaction isn't seen as a life-or-death scenario because if one deal falls off, you've got appointments on the books for more.

Now it's possible that you are reading this and you aren't new. Sometimes agents have a really great streak going and then, for one reason or another, land the plane. This means that it's not only new agents that have to build momentum. One day, because of a lack of prospecting or a sudden market shift or a personal adversity, you could find yourself sitting on the runway. If that happens, once again you'll need to take off into the wind. It's nothing to be ashamed of and you certainly won't be alone. What's great about planes (and agents) is that if you give them enough fuel, they'll always take off again, and again, and again. Just don't land your plane too much, okay? It's not the most enjoyable way to pilot your career.

Stage Two: Skill Building

Once you're consistently attending three appointments a week, you're in stage two of your transformation, and it's time to switch into skill building mode. That doesn't mean you forget how you soared to cruising altitude. It means you keep your lead generation going while deliberately working on your sales skills. How long you stay at stage two is entirely dependent on your own style of learning. There's no length of time to shoot for and no need to compare yourself to others. You'll develop at your own pace, and expectations from others will simply frustrate you. Skill building is about spending time on task and, frankly, it's not that sexy.

To set your expectations, this won't happen quickly. You'll spend three to five years with your head down improving your skill. It's called paying your dues and there's no way around it no matter what a random tech company of the day says to you in their marketing. At this stage, it's important to work hard on your business and go easy on yourself.

When skill building, there is naturally a lot of winning and even more losing. That's good, though, because you learn from the failures, not the wins. More specifically, you learn after a failure, when you make adjustments and try again. Clearly you can't do that if you don't schedule appointments regularly.

Your sales methodologies take center stage here. You'll work to get really good at moving people through the conversion chain, controlling your appointments, handling objections, and getting signatures. This is also where you develop a deep understanding of the four offers, which I discussed in the previous chapter. Through your sales magnets and direct marketing, you'll continually improve your offers to connect with new people. You'll spend a lot of time refining your follow-up efforts and building ever stronger relationships within your book of business.

In short, you'll be working every day to get better at persuading people.

After every appointment, step aside before the next task and review your performance while it's fresh in your head. Keep a skill building journal and note what you did well and where you got off track. It won't take long for you to notice patterns, and then, if you do have a coach, your work with him or her will be more effective. In fact, a productive way to zero in on your skills development is to track a few numbers. If you generate a good amount of leads and talk to plenty of people but don't schedule enough appointments, that's a clear sign you should work on using sales magnets to generate leads and appointments.

If you are going on appointments but aren't converting enough of them, then you'll need to analyze where you are weaker on appointments. Look at your entire process—from taking control to finding the problem to solving the problem to closing and handling objections. That's a mouthful but somewhere in there are the skills that need more development.

Or let's say you're able to get listings but they aren't selling. That's when you'll need to zero in on how you're presenting price and make sure you're taking listings at prices that will cause them to sell. If you're struggling here, odds are you've mutually agreed to take on listings you shouldn't have.

Along the way, you'll be working to keep your business macros in balance. That's not to say you'll always be in perfect balance. There are times during the year when our diets can go astray, like the holiday season or special occasions like birthdays. But once you learn how to control macronutrients in your diet, you can always get yourself back in balance. The same is true for your business. You may stray away from the basics at times and get lost in the highly addictive world of marketing tactics, but you'll be able to catch yourself before too much damage is done and make the necessary adjustments.

One day you'll be jamming along working on your skills and realize you're getting pretty good at selling. You'll know you've made it when you discover after an appointment that you were working with your methodologies unconsciously. It's one of the best feelings in the world and means you've reached the next stage.

Stage Three: Living the Top Producer Life

After building momentum and skill, top producers focus on living from mastery. Living from mastery isn't the same as living as a master. The former keeps you humble and in growth mode, ensuring long-term success. The latter is all about the ego and puts people at great risk of finding themselves at a dead stop on the runway.

You will find clear examples of both all around you. Odds are you can think of several people who are seen as very successful in your market or even in your own company whose practice seems to be one long episode of the me show. Their marketing is all about their image and they often jump at the chance to speak to other agents. When they do, what you'll hear is a bunch of stories about all of the tactics that have worked for them lately. Those in attendance applaud and eagerly ask questions about those tactics while feeding the ego of the supposed master.

It should make sense to you now why this happens and why it's so addictive. Tactics are just a bunch of sugar and carbs, and it's natural for ambitious and eager salespeople to want the quick sugar high. Even the energy these folks put off is addictive. You'll definitely feel excited around them, but once they walk away, you'll be left wondering what happened and question if you learned anything tangible you could actually go do yourself.

Sadly, I've seen too many people idolize those living as a master, not even realizing they might form another opinion if they got a chance to see what was going on behind the curtain. All of that energy used to create an image is an attempt to hide their own insecurities and is rooted deep within their subconscious mind.

For most people, I believe it takes a combination of a world-class coach or mentor and an act of grace to break loose of that energetic pattern. In astrology it's called Chiron (a wound you are born with), and astrologists believe everyone comes into the world with one. They believe it's our work in the world to discover it and work toward transforming it into energy that is healed and frees us up to use our full potential to help others with our talents. I really love the idea of that concept.

You can also look around and see people running their business and living their lives from mastery. These are the agents who are always in the top ranks of production. They may not always be number one, but they are never far off no matter what the market is doing because they always create their own market.

Real estate has not taken over their entire identity, and so the energy you feel from them is different. I'd argue that folks living from mastery have done plenty of work on their Chiron even if they don't understand it in those terms. And you'll probably hear about it because they aren't afraid to show you their warts. They are open about their failures because they know they wouldn't be where they are without them. They understand adversity for what it is and use it as a tool to reach their goals.

If you approach a person living from mastery, it's likely they are going to ask about you rather than talk about themselves. If you ask them for help, they'll respond by trying to get to the root of the problem before they offer any advice. In other words, they'll do for you just what they do for their clients: take control, find your problem, offer a solution, and then close. In this case, their close will likely come in the form of an inspiring challenge and a request to report back.

Nothing is more fulfilling for someone living from mastery than hearing back from a person they have worked to help. The results, positive or negative, are largely irrelevant. It's the feedback they most want because it lets them know their efforts mattered.

When you live from mastery, you'll find enjoyment in going deeper and asking why all this stuff works. You'll want to look for nuance in everything you do. Because you don't have to consciously think about your business macros anymore, you'll have the mental bandwidth to observe people on a deeper level while you're leading them through appointments.

This is why I'd recommend always having a journal close by, especially when you're operating at this level. When you notice what others don't and take the time to fuss over them in your journal, you're allowing your brain the chance to perform highly creative functions. You'll slowly develop the ability to connect dots that others can't. You'll find yourself adding to the knowledge passed down to you by your teachers and mentors. In fact, one of the best ways to honor your mentors is to surpass them.

If you're lucky enough to find a mentor who celebrates your success and seems to get more excited about them than you do, stay as close to that person for as long as you can.

8

What To Do When
You Fall Off Track

Declare a Day One

If you ever get too far off track, there's a simple trick to instantly stop any more damage from being done. It's called declaring a day one, which represents the energy of your first day in business before anything went wrong and you were full of wide-eyed optimism. Sometimes people forget that, when you're the boss, you have the power to start over at any time. Over the years, I've started over a ton. Sometimes twice in one week.

THE DAY ONE FORMULA

▶ **Interrupt the pattern**. There is a reason most people start new stuff like diets, workouts, and business ideas on Mondays. It's a good day to break an old pattern by starting a new one.

▶ **Lift your head and look further out**. Why do you want to change? You got lost in a bit of drama, so what? That's already in the past. What is your big why? Are you in real estate to pay off debt? Invest? Secure your retirement? Get off the day-to-day for a moment and reconnect to why you got into this business in the first place.

- **Recommit to a goal.** This could be as simple as writing out a clear and concise statement about what you wish to accomplish by the end of the year and what will happen in your life when you do.

- **Take an honest look at where you are.** For example, if you started the year with a goal of $10 million in volume and are sitting at $5 million now, spend some time thinking about exactly what would be required to bridge that gap.

- **Make a decision.** Are you willing to do what it takes to bridge the gap? Sometimes the answer is yes, sometimes no. Either way, make the decision. If the decision is no, it's time to set a new short-term goal to get you to the end of the year (which is November 30 in our industry because most of what you put under contract in December closes the next year).

- **Make your declaration and forget the past.** Let go of the past and move forward. Declare the day a day one.

- **Start where you are.** Do you have one listing? Fine, start there and make sure you have it positioned to sell. One buyer client? Okay, get them into the office. Got nothing but a bunch of names in your book of business? All right, pick up the phone and start having conversations. Stay focused and build from there.

HONOR THE ENERGY OF THE DAY

As long as we are talking about days, let's talk about the unique energy of each day. This is a concept that occurred to me after many years of taking Sunday as my day off. That day took on an incredibly distinct energy that was different than Sundays in the past.

As I got better at controlling my days such that I truly enjoyed the freedom that comes with being self-employed, each day of the week took on its own energy. I'll describe each day here to inspire you to think about what each day means to you. Our time is our life and so thinking about the energy of each day and how you will spend your time hits at the very essence of designing your life as a top producer.

I wouldn't expect you to design your days exactly like mine—after all, you may not want Sunday off. Maybe Friday is the day you want to escape work. Use my preferences as a model to design yours.

MONDAY ENERGY: BUILDING MOMENTUM

I've never been one to dread Monday. There have only been a few short periods of time when I resisted working on Monday. It happened when I needed to change the work, not the day.

Monday is the day to get your mind back in the game and it's always a little intense. It helps that most other people are doing the same even if they aren't bringing conscious awareness to it. Because of what you'll read on Friday and Sunday, Monday is both intense and inspiring. I typically rocket right into the week with no hesitation because I love my chosen work and I love the people I get to serve.

I can't stress this enough: if you can't say those things about your profession, drop all of this and make finding work you look forward to your only point of focus. The only way I know to do that is to try out lots of different jobs until you find your inspiration. Sometimes, once we make it past our twenties, we impose unnecessary expectations on ourselves and suffer in work that we really don't like. If we insist that everyone progresses in their careers at the same general pace, not much space is left for experimentation beyond your first serious career. I'm sure that way of thinking is a big contributing factor to a midlife crisis.

TUESDAY ENERGY: PEDAL TO THE METAL

When I started in business as a young agent, Tuesday was highly structured. It began with a sales meeting, then property tour, which went through noon. After that it was a mad dash to squeeze in as much as I could by the end of the day. I no longer do sales meetings and tours on Tuesday (neither does anyone else really) but the energy remains. I love Tuesday because if you build momentum on Monday, you can really floor it and be super productive.

WEDNESDAY ENERGY: HEAD DOWN, STAY FOCUSED

Wednesday might be the most unremarkable of the days in the week. It's also potentially the most powerful.

While some people celebrate hump day as the halfway point to the weekend, or pre-pre Friday, I've learned to milk it for all the production I can. Monday's momentum building and Tuesday's pedal to the medal spirit lead us to a day where, if we keep our head down and remain focused, we can make some serious progress. It's sort of like when a plane has made it to cruising altitude, it makes the greatest amount of progress with the least amount of effort.

THURSDAY ENERGY:
SEATBACK UP, FINAL APPROACH

When you're having a good week, Thursday can be really fulfilling. For me it's the last full day of production and the day to wrap up the work I set out to accomplish at the beginning of the week.

Thursday usually comes with an energy of cooperation, especially toward the end of the day. Most people are trying to finish up as much as possible to prevent their work from bleeding into Friday night. Even if they just got it together on Wednesday, people are typically focused. In my experience, Thursday is the day I'm most likely to get people I'm working with to deliver on projects.

FRIDAY ENERGY: REVIEW AND REGROUP

Friday is the day to work *on* my business after spending four days working *in* it. No one makes consistent progress toward goals by working day-in-day-out without regular periods of review. My Friday always starts with a short period of time to finish up work I wasn't able to get done by Thursday. That's followed by an extensive weekly review.

The review is a chance for me to clear my emails, make sure I've responded to everyone, and think about what I've done. After that I'm able to determine my intentions for the next week. Once my intentions are set, all of the tasks I need to do get time blocked on the calendar.

This is key to relieving Sunday evening stress over work. When you already know what you're going to do Monday morning, there's not much to worry about. In fact, no successful self-employed person shows up for work Monday morning wondering what they'll do that week.

I usually finish the review between noon and 1:00 p.m. and then spend the afternoon with the pups and ease into date night.

SATURDAY ENERGY: ACTIVE AND FUN

I never sleep in on the weekend. It's not good for your health and seems like a waste of time anyway. Also I'm not twenty. Instead, I'm at the gym early, often the first one there. Then it's off to the farmers market and spending the afternoon on dog walks and personal projects.

And I never wanted to be the old dude in the club (not that I was ever a club kid) so most Saturday nights are spent with good food and drinks. When I was an active agent, instead of going to the farmers market, I'd spend Saturday showing houses. That was the time I reserved to meet new buyer clients for their consultations and showings. If I was showing homes on a weekday, it was to buyers who were already clients still looking for the right home.

SUNDAY ENERGY: SELF-CARE

If you've ever worked with me, you know I'm impossible to reach on Sunday. That's because as a young man I was taught to take at least one full day off from work each week in order to recharge.

As my business grew, the day began to represent far more than just recharging for work on Monday. It allowed space for other interests so my identity didn't become totally defined by my career. Self-employed people who never allow themselves to develop into well-rounded humans are not only boring to be around, but usually don't even realize their refusal to let go of work is a clear sign of scarcity-based thinking.

The Congruence Checklist, Your Personal Top Producer Life Checklist

If the story in your head is that you are a successful agent but you aren't doing the things that a successful agent does, you can quickly get to a point where you are pummeling yourself internally. This goes way beyond the money.

For example, for a new agent who happens to have a lot of wealth in their life—either because of family money, prior career successes, or a high-earning spouse—other agents tend to think they're fine whether they sell a house or not. And while it's true in cases like this that the agent won't need commissions to put food on the table or buy another horse and more diamonds, they need it for congruence. In other words, congruence isn't about money, it's about respecting yourself for how you're showing up in the world.

Beyond money, success means proving yourself and making a contribution to society. When a person is out of congruence with themselves, there are only two options: (1) change the story in your head and give up on the goals you said you wanted to do or be and have or (2) find where you are out of congruence with yourself and shore it up. That's why I created the congruence checklist here. Use it when a deep gut check is in order and make sure you're in congruence with each item.

✔ HOW YOU THINK

You get what you think about whether you want it or not. Are your thoughts dominated by how nice it will feel when you accomplish your goals or do you constantly dwell on what's missing? Every level of growth requires a new level of thinking. Have you upgraded your thinking to support your current vision?

✔ HOW YOU RUN YOUR DAY

Thinking big and acting small is the same as thinking small. If you haven't taken control of your days, you're living out other people's agenda by default. Typically people who have a sort of stubborn refusal to control their own day have fears to overcome relating to their vision. If you feel you've got your mindset under control yet can't seem to control your time, go back to mindset and find the fears that you are allowing to stop you from living out your agenda.

✔ RESPECT FOR YOUR CRAFT

Do you believe in what you do and that it's a beneficial service for our society? Do you see selling as an art form that is to be studied, honored, and respected? Do you spend enough time working on your craft or do you hope deals will fall into your lap and work out perfectly?

✔ WHAT YOU ARE WORTH

Are you charging what you are worth? In real estate, are you charging full commission or do you discount just to get business?

✔ WHO IS YOUR IDEAL CLIENT?

Have you done the work to gain clarity about your ideal client? How often do you revisit and refine your client avatar—the representation of your ideal client? When you feel off, how quickly can you think of your avatar and spring back to life? If you've never been through an exercise to create a client avatar, visit the bonus section at jasenedwards.com/TPLBonus

✔ USING YOUR VOICE

Have you come out from behind the listing? Do you have something to say other than "I'm an agent, please use me"? Have you taken the time lately to express your opinions and provide context to people you serve or have you mindlessly flooded them with more information?

✔ YOUR BIG WHY

Do you know why you're going to work every day? Is your life all about work for work's sake or is work serving the bigger picture of the life you wish to design? Have you forgotten that, as a self-employed person, designing your own life is literally required for success?

✔ KICKING YOUR OWN BUTT

One of the hallmarks of a person who is living the Top Producer Life is their ability to kick their own butt. Countless trainers and coaches in the real estate industry sell the promise that if you take their program, or enroll in their coaching program, they'll hold you accountable. The problem is that they can't do that, only you can.

Whenever you see a testimonial or a case study where credit is given to the coach for holding them accountable, you can be sure what you're really seeing is someone who has the ability to kick their own butt. That person would have stayed accountable to themselves no matter who they hired as their coach. And that's the key: they are accountable to themselves.

Accountability is an inside job and long term. You can only remain accountable to yourself, not a coach. Top producers understand that when they have clarity about why they are in business, accountability takes care of itself. If you ever find yourself struggling with accountability, the solution is to find clarity in your big why. Never approach coaching and training programs expecting them to provide something they can't ever give you. For top producers, training and coaching is about challenging you to think and act bigger. Accountability is assumed.

After going through those items, you no doubt have identified where your weak spots are. They'll likely change every time you go through the checklist because each time you do so, you'll have grown into a new version of yourself. Take the observations you make about yourself and flip back to the appropriate business macro and dig in. The answers are there for you. Real estate isn't always easy, but it also isn't that complicated.

Trust Life

Have you ever gone through adversity and, when the storm was over, looked back only to understand why it was exactly what you needed at the time? These days I believe we are always experiencing just what we need at every moment. In other words, I've learned to trust life.

That's not to say that I haven't ever fought against life. I'm a Capricorn after all and have the ability to stubbornly fight against life until it almost destroys me. I learned that the hard way in my personal life. When it came to business, in my twenties and thirties I had big goals but hadn't fully learned that every adversity I faced was life's way of trying to help. I didn't understand that I'd attracted that adversity through my desires for an improved life. So I thought the right thing to do was push against adversity and try to prevent as much of it as possible.

When you got into real estate, you started a journey of transformation that won't always be easy. Working for yourself in commission-only sales forces you to deal with all of the deep personal issues that corporate 9-to-5 employees have the luxury of ignoring. But make no mistake about it, life heard your wishes for more and is busy lining up all kinds of adversity for you to handle. You wouldn't be here if all you wanted was to survive. You were surviving before you got into real estate and that means you want more.

As you work on the concepts in this book, try to remember that, and one day you too will welcome adversity as the friendly helper it is designed to be.

At the end of the day, this is supposed to be fun. If you're like I was at first and don't quite trust life yet, maybe you can trust me. If you sense that I've written every word to help you along your path of transformation, then repeat this in your mind over and over until you believe it: life is always working out for me.

9

The Twenty-Two-Year
Listing Appointment

It was a hot Sunday at the end of August in Austin, and I was walking around Town Lake trail with my partner, Jon, and our dog, Chug. At the time, I was running a small independent brokerage when the office called. I didn't answer because it was my day off and everyone knew it. They also knew they could call as much as they wanted and leave me messages, but they remembered I wouldn't even hear the messages until Monday.

But this time they didn't leave a message. They called again and again and again and again. I started to get angry and asked Jon if he would mind if I answered the phone. My plan was to get whoever was calling back in line because clearly they had lost their mind.

The next time the phone rang, I answered and the agent was super apologetic but told me there was a man in the office who refused to leave until he spoke to me. When they said the guy's name, I knew instantly who was there. The man in the lobby was named Doug, and he had been my first real listing appointment twenty-two years earlier. When I was learning how to prospect and schedule listing appointments, he was the first person to give me a real appointment. By that I mean when I called, he was actually thinking of selling and he was also willing to meet with me.

I still had a ton to learn about selling and the listing appointment itself, but Doug was super patient with me and let me go through the whole presentation. I think he did that because he was a salesperson too. He sold telecom equipment for AT&T. But he didn't hire me to sell his house that day. He listed with someone else.

I realized we went to the same gym. So several times a week, when I'd see him there, I was reminded of that rough first appointment. It took several months before I stopped feeling self-conscious when we passed each other.

Life went on and we both found success in our careers. He moved several times and never was a client of mine, but on this hot Sunday he was in my lobby, his listing had just expired, and he was looking for my help.

I've always maintained my license for personal use but wasn't taking real estate clients at that point because I had plenty on my plate running the brokerage. Plus, I didn't want to be seen as a competitor to my own agents. But Doug was insistent I come see his house and talk to him, and I could tell he wouldn't take no for an answer.

The next week when I met him, he told me he was suffering from a serious form of brain cancer and didn't have much time left. He owned his house free and clear and was selling so he could use the cash to check off items on his bucket list before he made his transition. These words are forever burned into my brain: "Jasen, you are the only person I trust to sell my house. Will you help me?"

What's interesting about this story is that I was never able to develop a consistent business relationship with Doug over the years. He was on my mailing and email lists the whole time, but we rarely if ever communicated after that first appointment years ago. What's more, the home he wanted me to sell was in a super hot area of Austin in a strong seller's market. In my opinion, the only reason his home didn't sell with the other agent was because Doug and his last home were here to teach me a lesson.

After I had twenty-two years in the business, Doug taught me more than anyone else how important it is to treat salesmanship with respect. He taught me more than any other client how profoundly we affect the lives of our clients, and he taught me how critical and urgent it is for everyone in this business to do the deep personal work necessary to overcome our limiting beliefs, drop concern over what other people think, develop our salesmanship skills, and use our voices to serve the marketplace.

Doug's properties were both the first listing I didn't get and the last listing I ever took. He died about six months after we went to closing, but the energy of his lesson lives on. And in a way, what he taught me was the culmination of an education in sales that started when I was six years old and picked up my dad's book *See You at the Top* by Zig Ziglar. The most profound lesson in that book is that you can get anything out of life that you want, as long as you first help enough other people get what they want.

Now go build your own Top Producer Life.

Acknowledgments

I've loved books since I was a kid. While my friends would play video games, I'd gravitate toward books, *See You at the Top* by Zig Ziglar being the one I remember most. I always knew I'd write at least one book and successfully avoided the challenge for years, using my perceived difficulty of the process as the excuse.

It turns out, while writing this book was a challenge, it wasn't difficult. Every time I was asked why I hadn't written a book, I would secretly beat myself up for not having done it. Now I can see clearly that life was guiding me all along. I suppose I can't speak for fiction, but I believe a nonfiction book must be earned by the author. Life needed time to teach me, through personal experience, so that later on it could channel this message through me.

At the beginning of 2020 my goal was to complete the first draft of the manuscript by the end of the year. Now we'll all look back on this time and reflect on our quarantine projects as the world dealt with the COVID-19 pandemic. This book was my quarantine project, and not only did it help me retain my sanity, it taught me that I love writing as much as I already love speaking from the stage.

As this book was being written and produced, I rode a roller coaster of emotions. During the highs I experienced inspiration in its purest form, a feeling of being in-spirit, directly connected to source energy. During the low moments, I experienced incredible amounts of self-doubt and intense imposter syndrome. However, whatever emotion presented itself on any given day, I always felt guided and loved by people living and transitioned.

Thank you first to my dad and to Dr. Wayne Dyer and Zig Ziglar. These three gentlemen spoke to me energetically from another plane of existence at the perfect time and delivered the guidance I needed to write.

Thank you to my unofficial support gang who showed enthusiasm from the moment I said I was writing and showed up unannounced with messages of encouragement when they had no clue how badly they were needed. Alphabetically so you don't fight: Isabel Affinito, Mary Ann Burke, Amanda Cowan, Rose Hayden, Katherine Johnson, JJ Kennemer, Alex Marquez, Mallory Mundy, and Kasia Olek.

Thank you to my spiritual guide and my sister, in basically every way you can define the word, Lisa Shelton. I may rebel against your guidance frequently (isn't that what a little brother is supposed to do?), but the messages always get through. Love you!

Thank you to my mom who is the ultimate supporter and single-handedly keeps Hallmark in business. Your courage and unbreakable spirit will always inspire and guide me.

Thank you to my mentors who have helped shape my career since high school: Ron Redder, Chris Heagerty, Floyd Wickman, Mary Johnson, Vanessa Bivens, and Sherry Lewis.

And finally, thank you to my family, Jon, Chug, and Hugo, for believing in me more than I believe in myself. You are what makes living our own Top Producer Life worthwhile. I love you.

About the Author

Jasen Edwards started learning about sales and real estate while in high school. He dropped out of college after a few semesters and got his license at the age of eighteen. During the first year and a half he only made one sale and $6,000 in commission. Then, out of desperation, he enrolled in a three-month sales training program where he was taught the art of salesmanship. He outproduced his entire office during the program and earned ten times what he had to that point.

Jasen spent over a decade selling homes in Austin, Texas, was the youngest person ever listed on the *Austin Business Journal's* Top 50 agents list, and was featured on the cover of *REALTOR Magazine* before he turned thirty.

He became the go-to guy in his company for agents needing help with their business and decided to become a coach and motivational speaker. Jasen mentored under industry legend and Hall of Fame speaker, Floyd Wickman, and earned the rank of Master Trainer. He's traveled the US and worked with agents in every market you can imagine; from white hot seller's markets, to the extreme buyer's market of the great recession.

Jasen spent several years being mentored by self-help guru and "father of inspiration," Dr. Wayne Dyer, who encouraged him to write.

Over the past eighteen years, Jasen has taught thousands of salespeople the art of salesmanship, helped them reach top producer status, and inspired them to achieve their individual vision for a successful career in real estate. His clients do what most think is impossible: they charge above-average commissions, enjoy regular time off, and experience the freedom they dreamed of when they first got licensed.

Jasen lives his own version of a Top Producer Life in Southern California with his partner, Jon, and their dogs Chug and Hugo.

Made in the USA
Middletown, DE
13 June 2021